UNDER THE BLACK GUM TREE: 165 YEARS IN THE PINEY WOODS

WINNIE GRAHAM

STEPHEN F. AUSTIN STATE UNIVERSITY PRESS
NACOGDOCHES ♦ TEXAS

Copyright © 2013 by Winnie Graham. All rights reserved. Printed in the United States of America. No part of this book may be used or reproduced in any manner whatsoever without writter permission except in the case of brief quotations embodied in critical articles or reviews.

For more informaion:
Stephen F. Austin State University Press
P.O. Box 13007 SFA Station
Nacogdoches, Texas 75962
sfapress@sfasu.edu
sfasu.edu/sfapress

Book Design: Laura Davis

Distributed by Texas A&M University Press Consortium
www.tamupress.com
1.800.826.8911

LIBRARY OF CONGRESS CATALOGING-IN-PUBLICATION DATA

Graham, Winnie
Under the Blackgum Tree / Winnie Graham - 1st ed.

p.cm.

ISBN-13: 978-1-62288-022-5

1. Memoir. 2. Texas - Folklore. 3. Texas - Piney Woods.

CONTENTS

PROLOGUE: THE PINEY WOODS: A DAB OF HISTORY ⊗ **9**
    1. The Black-eyed Pea/Pinto Bean Divide ⊗ **15**
    2. A Terrapin's Pace ⊗ **18**
    3. Some Do's and Don'ts ⊗ **21**

#1 UNDER THE BLACKGUM: HOG HUNTING ⊗ **24**
    4. The Early Settlers: Grandpa's Lineage ⊗ **26**
        James Eason and Caroline Welch Russell
        William D. Russell (Grandpa Bill)
        Mary Chestnut Russell

2#2 UNDER THE BLACKGUM: HOW UNCLE BUD GOT HIS NAME ⊗ **36**
    5. The Early Settlers: Grandma's Lineage ⊗ **37**
        The Renfros
        The Browns
    6. Granny Hutch and Her Two Husbands ⊗ **42**
        John E. Brown and Aaron Hutchinson

#3 UNDER THE BLACKGUM: A BONE FELON TALE ⊗ **47**
    7. That Old Time Religion ⊗ **48**
    8. The Church in the Wildwood ⊗ **51**

#4 UNDER THE BLACKGUM: CHURCH TALES ⊗ **56**
    9. Grandma Wade and Some of Her Husbands ⊗ **58**

#5 UNDER THE BLACKGUM: GRANDMA WADE'S VERSES AND SAYINGS ⊗ **65**
    10. Leah Azeta Sowell Russell: Her Growing-Up Years ⊗ **67**
    11. William Eli Russell: His Growing-Up Years ⊗ **70**
    12. Riding the Ring ⊗ **73**
    13. Eli's and Leah's Young Family ⊗ **77**

#6 UNDER THE BLACKGUM: IN THE FUST AND FO'MST PLACE ∞ 84
    14. Vittles and Grub ∞ **85**
    15. Step-ins and Duds ∞ **93**
    16. Lillian Leaves the Nest ∞ **100**
    17. Fred Graham ∞ **112**
    18. The Ferris Wheel Ride ∞ **132**

#7 UNDER THE BLACKGUM: THE TRUNK IN THE GARAGE ∞ 129
    19. The Pine Grove ∞ **133**
    20. Fiddling Around ∞ **138**
    21. Back at the House ∞ **147**
    22. Grandma Wade's Fourth Husband ∞ **156**

#8 UNDER THE BLACKGUM: UNCLE JOSH IN THE CORRAL ∞ 159
    23. The Dipping Vat ∞ **161**
    24. Uncle Thedford ∞ **167**
    25. Grandma's Favorite Things ∞ **171**

#9 UNDER THE BLACKGUM: CORNY JOKES ∞ 177
    26. The Great Dispersal ∞ **179**
    27. Some More Peanuts ∞ **186**
    28. A Visit to Jonesville ∞ **190**

#10 UNDER THE BLACKGUM: MAMA'S WORDS OF WISDOM ∞ 196
    29. A Cabin in the Woods ∞ **198**

    Acknowledgments ∞ **201**

In memory of
JCE

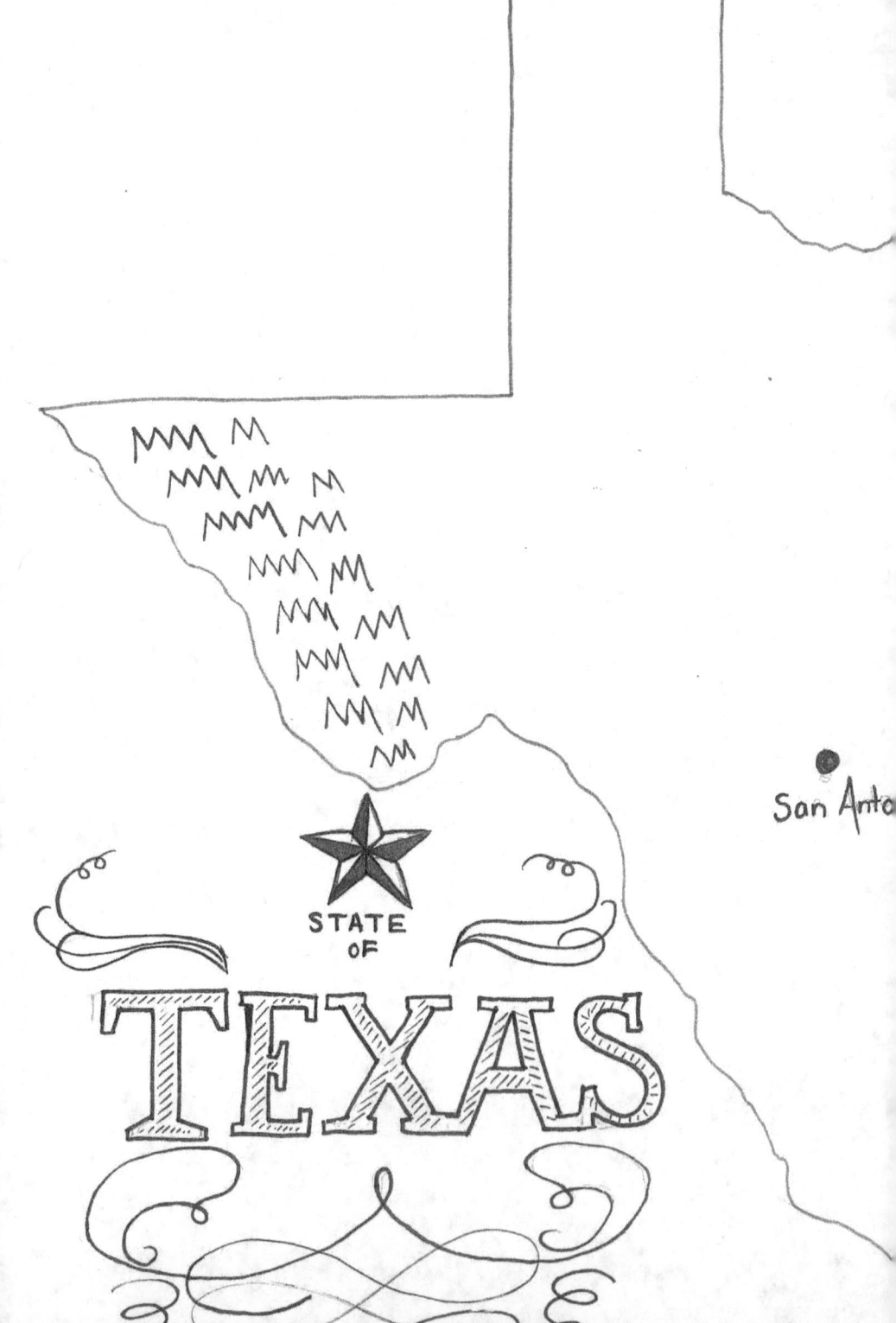

Prologue:

The Piney Woods: A Dab of History

It's March and a light breeze stirs the wildflowers that are just beginning to bloom. Yellow jasmine vines and wild grapes twining up many of the trees have started budding out, and the dogwood and redbud trees are getting ready to bloom. In the river bottoms the wild evergreen magnolias and holly show sprigs of new growth. The scent of pine needles and pine rosin is strong in the warm air. The deciduous trees in the woods — elm, sweet gum (liquid amber), hickory, several species of oak, along with the wild plums and persimmons — are beginning to leaf out. Some of the blackberry brambles and huckleberry bushes already have some green leaves. Winter, with its frosty mornings and occasional freezing nights, is over and the heat and humidity of summer are a good ways off. If you pick up a handful of dirt, you'll find that the soil gives off more heat to your skin than it draws out. It's time to go fishing, plant gardens and fields, and gather a mess of wild poke greens for a salad.

These are the Piney Woods of East Texas that the early American pioneers found, and of which vast stretches still remain. The word "Texas" often conjures up images of sagebrush and cactus or wild chaparral, but that description fits the Piney Woods about as well as a Hawaiian rainforest scenario would fit Manhattan Island. Technically a mixed hardwood/softwood forest, pines do predominate. Some of the once-plentiful hardwood trees still remain, but many have been logged off over the years.

The area gets decent rainfall (except in drought years), so rivers, creeks, and branches wind through the countryside. According to tradition, a branch empties into a creek, and a creek into a river.

In the 1820s, the first settlers from the U.S. began arriving in Texas, which then belonged to Mexico. By 1835, the "Texians," as they were then called, had become numerous enough to get uppity with the Mexican government and declare their independence. The rest, as the saying goes, is history: the Alamo, the Battle of San Jacinto, etc. Then, as more pioneers and newborn babies increased the population, more settlements were established. By the time of the Civil War, (the early 1860s), small towns had sprung up here and there. A few towns grew enough to become small cities, but really big cities, Houston and Beaumont for instance, which both had streetcars by the time of the Civil War, lie on the outer fringes of the Piney Woods.

Cotton was the main farm crop until along about World War II, when cotton grown on irrigated fields in the arid Southwest became cheaper. A lot of Piney Woods farmers then started raising beef cattle. Corn, sorghum, other grains, and hay were always grown to feed folks' milk cows, hogs, and chickens, as were big patches of black-eyed peas and vegetables for the table.

Beginning in the early 1900s, lumbering became a big moneymaking enterprise. Well, not always moneymaking for everyone. Within a few years, sawmill operations phased over from farm-based affairs to self-contained lumber mill towns complete with commissaries and company-owned houses for workers' families. At many of the big mills the workers were paid in script that they then spent for coffee, flour, shoes, etc., at the commissary. Many young farm "boys" worked as sawyers, "flatheads," or muleskinners, and often "batched" (that is, lived as bachelors) in makeshift cabins in the woods. Most of them hoped to be able to save the 40 dollars or so it took to buy a piece of farmland, and many did. Others spent their lives logging or working in the mills.

The "oil bidness" is, of course, a trademark of Texas. In East Texas the major oilfields are along the Gulf coast to the south in the Beaumont area, and to the north in the Tyler area. Something about the geology of the deep East Texas Piney Woods, which lie between, didn't lend itself to petroleum formation. Extensive deposits of lignite coal are known to exist, and possibly deep deposits of natural gas, but oil deposits are scarce as cactus. East Texans, however, have still played a major role in the "oil bidness" since about World War I. Oil field pumping units built by the Lufkin Foundry can be seen by the thousands in oil fields all over the world. They're easy to spot: the word "Lufkin" is embossed conspicuously on their upper crossbeam.

Most of the family farms have now become country retirement homes, often with their former cotton and cornfields planted in pine trees for timber. The old sawmill towns withered away after World War II, and have been replaced by a few industrial-like lumber plants.

Through it all though, in many ways the Piney Woods has not changed. If the earliest pioneers could come back, they would recognize the settlements and back roads they helped establish and the county seat's courthouse square. They would recognize the last names of many families as that of their own or that of their friends and neighbors. They would note that folks with some of these last names still live in their families' original settlements. And they would still see Piney Woods stretching out over every horizon.

REPUBLIC OF TEXAS DOLLAR BILL

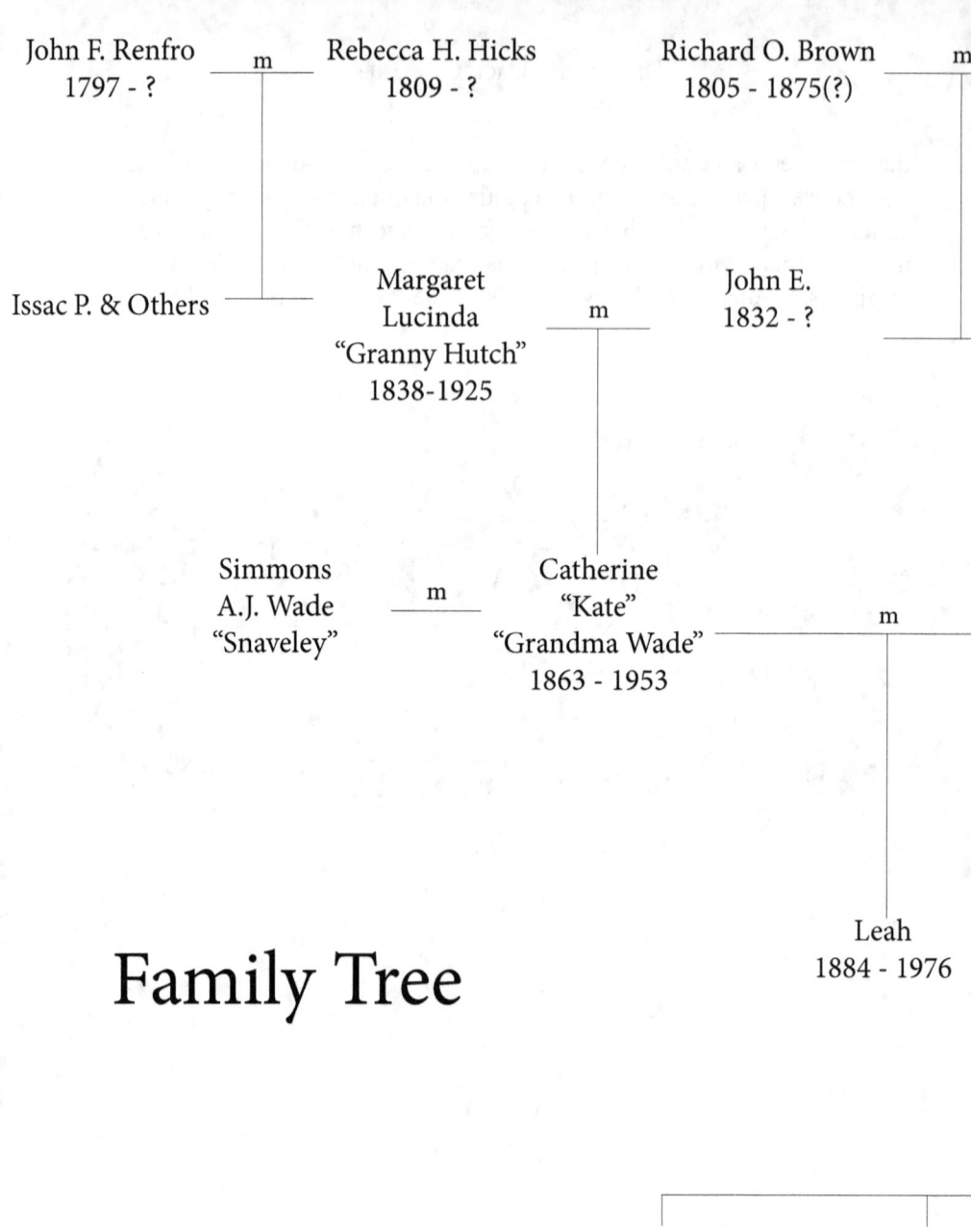

Family Tree

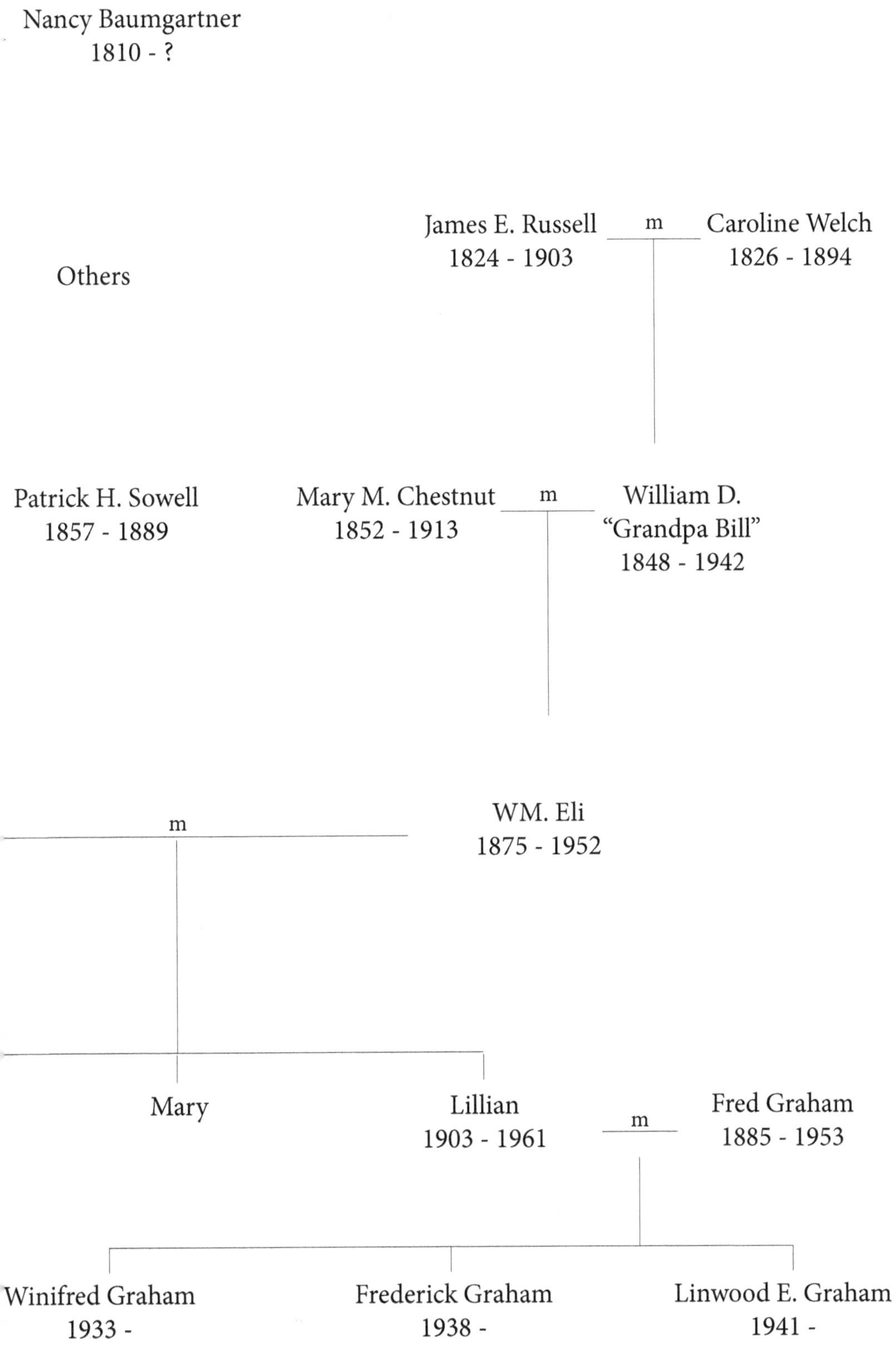

Nancy Baumgartner
1810 - ?

Others

James E. Russell   m   Caroline Welch
1824 - 1903   1826 - 1894

Patrick H. Sowell   Mary M. Chestnut   m   William D.
1857 - 1889   1852 - 1913   "Grandpa Bill"
                                                           1848 - 1942

m   WM. Eli
       1875 - 1952

Mary   Lillian   m   Fred Graham
           1903 - 1961   1885 - 1953

Winifred Graham   Frederick Graham   Linwood E. Graham
1933 -   1938 -   1941 -

1
THE BLACK-EYED PEA/PINTO BEAN DIVIDE

On the eastern side of Texas an imaginary broad and squiggly boundary marks what I call the black-eyed pea/pinto bean divide. Within this area, folks young and old have long been nourished on black-eyed peas. From family dining tables to roadside cafes you'll be served black-eyed peas — always with cornbread and often with fried chicken or catfish. In the rest of Texas and farther to the west, you can expect pinto beans and barbecued brisket, or maybe refried beans (pintos again) and *chalupas*.

In the east-west direction, this divide runs from the state line with Louisiana (the Sabine river) to about the outer eastern edge of Houston. In the other direction, it runs through along about Beaumont in the south, and about 100 miles or so below Dallas in the north. It encircles roughly 20,000 square miles, just a tad smaller than Scotland.

This area containing the Piney Woods of East Texas forms part of the transition between the Deep South and the American West. Piney Woods folks tend to be sort of Southern (hence the black-eyed peas), but they don't fit that mold very well. They fit the Western mold even less (hence only occasional pinto beans). And the relatively recent mold of the typical Texan fits a lot of them now, as it would have the earlier settlers, about like a new, unbroken-in pair of shoes. They are, in short, what I call Piney Woodsians.

My Piney Woods lineage dates back to 1838 when one bunch of my predecessors migrated from Tennessee. The next bunch came from Missouri in 1839, then another from Arkansas in 1853. They all settled in and procreated in Old Testament quantities. By the time of Mama's childhood in the early 1900s, she had kinfolks behind every tree.

From the earliest settlers until about the mid-1950s, folks in my family, and many, many other families, lived on small farms. Their lives revolved around farm work, family, and church. Typical of farm families across the U.S. in those days, they worked to produce their own food and feed and to eke out enough cash to pay for the few items that had to be store-bought. Family ties and religion, along with black-eyed peas, were more typically Southern.

Like Southerners and other Texans, Piney Woodsians — except for a sourpuss here and there — have always loved to laugh. Till this good day you'll hear folks laughing about as often as you hear them call each other "y'all." Also, most of them, including my kinfolks past and present, got inoculated along with their mother's milk with a knack for telling tales.

I originally started out to write down a few of my family's tales for our current generation, but the Piney Woods kept butting in. That is, telling only about family would be about like serving black-eyed peas without cornbread. So, while this memoir is built around my family's tales and history, the Piney Woods lore and way of life, dating back to the earliest settlers, get their share of attention.

Most of the tales in these pages are cheerful since we were, and are, a jolly bunch. The grownups passed lots of the stories along as we sat on the porch or in front of the fireplace. They wedged in other shorter tales as folks took a break from work (often in my family) in the shade of the black gum tree.

Way back yonder, when my grandparents cleared the timber off their land for crops, Grandpa left a good-sized black gum tree growing in what would become the middle of his field. Over the next 50 years it shaded many a soul, from infants to the gray-haired or bewattled. At cotton-picking or corn-thinning time, folks took some quilts and a bucket, with its communal dipper, of cool water from the bottom of the well and set up a rest area beneath the tree. A girl too young to help out in the field minded the little young'uns as they napped and played on quilt pallets. During rest breaks, the men sat back and rolled a cigarette; the women took off their shoes and aired their feet.

Long ago, after a slow and natural old age, the tree met its demise. In its memory, I have titled some shorter pieces in these pages "Under the Black Gum."

From the earliest settlers until well into the 1900s, much of the Piney Woods remained an unchanged wilderness. It had neither the cleared acreages of sprawling ranches nor, except in a few cases, of large plantations. The land carved out for small farms speckled the Piney Woods expanse more like polka dots than parking lots. Beginning in the late 1800s, clear-cutting by timber companies did leave gaps in the woods. In the first half of the 1900s, several thousand square miles were set aside as National Forests.

In the olden days, the scattered farms seldom abutted one another.

Unlike farms in more intensively agricultural areas, the cultivated fields of very few families ended smack dab next to a neighbor's field. Instead, woods surrounded many farms on one or two sides, and sometimes on all four. Thus lots of Piney Woodsians lived day in and day out with the beauty and reality of undomesticated nature.

Along with all my other family traits and habits, my instinct for roaming around in the woods got implanted shortly after my pattycake days. Early on I tagged along on jaunts with the grownups. Then, after advancing to "expeditions" with other young'uns, I learned how to find my way around in the woods all by myself. I also learned not to corner any kind of wild animal, nor to traipse through a patch of stinging nettle.

These woods that we roamed were the very same ones my predecessors knew so well. Many generations ago, when these folks became Piney Woodsians, some put down their roots in Nacogdoches and San Augustine Counties. A bunch of the others, including Grandpa's grandpa and Grandma's great grandpa, settled in what is now Angelina County. They built their homesteads and planted their black-eyed pea patches several miles outside of what is now Huntington, which, in turn, is about 15 miles south of what is now Lufkin. They named their settlement Oak Flat, and we've had kinfolks there till this good day.

I never lived full time in Oak Flat until quite recently, but over my lifetime I've spent many a day, week, and month there. When my brothers and I got old enough, we stayed all summer with Grandma and Grandpa. We didn't think of their place as a second home, but rather as another first home. We roamed the woods, of course, and also earned our keep by helping out with farm work. I still own a parcel, as do my brothers, of what was once Grandpa's field where the black gum tree stood. It's also where I used to help thin corn and pick peas and go fetch a watermelon on a hot afternoon.

I've roamed a lot of woods, as well as other places, since then, and although I sometimes eat — and like — pinto beans, I still prefer black-eyed peas. We replanted pine trees on Grandpa's old field several years back. They're now sizable enough for yellow jasmines to begin twining up their trunks. Hardwood seeds blown in or dropped by birds have taken root and begun sprouting. Maybe at least one of the sprouts is a black gum. It would be fitting if some of our kinfolks yet to come along could sit in its shade.

2
A Terrapin's Pace

In the Piney Woods, time bumped forward at a terrapin's speed. While historical events made the news elsewhere, the frontier lifestyle lasted for almost 100 years for many families. And by "frontier lifestyle," I do not mean the macho, "shoot 'em up" Western movie type.

Electricity was not brought in until the mid-1950s. Almost no farmhouses had plumbing of any kind, indoors or out, until about that same time. Dirt roads, often impassable in winter, eventually replaced wagon tracks. But, even after horseless carriages became numerous elsewhere, very few Piney Woodsians owned one, so most traveled by horseback, wagon, or afoot anyway. Likewise, folks cultivated their fields with horse- and mule-drawn plows until after World War II when the few affluent farmers invested in tractors. Grandpa's mama was still spinning her own yarn until along about 1890.

The Piney Woods version of the English language harks back to an era even earlier than coal oil (kerosene) lamps. It evolved from the form of English spoken by British immigrants to the Atlantic coastal South as early as the 1600s. As pioneers pushed the U.S. frontier westward across the Appalachians and the Smokies, mile by mile, its "Britishness" became disguised by "Southernness." Various regions added touches of their own, but the language's ancestry has never been completely obliterated.

The Piney Woods version — a sort of Texanized Southern drawl sprinkled with lots of its own pronunciation and grammar — took root by at least the mid-1800s. Until my early adulthood, I heard it from one of my great grandfathers (born 1848) and a great grandmother (born 1863). And it has been passed along, minus very little, till this good day to many Piney Woodsians, including me.

Many words, some still commonly used, are listed as archaic or middle English in the dictionary: "blinky" milk, for instance, to denote milk that has gone a bit sour, and "vittles" (victuals), as in "the vittles are on the table." Two other words often used by the older folks are not even in the dictionary: "mought," used interchangeably with "might," as in "I mought go to town on Saturday," and "hope" as a past tense for the verb "help," as in "I hope him plant his corn."

The drawl allows folks plenty of pronunciation space to add syllables to a word or replace a crisp sounding letter with a softer one. For instance, the word "smooth" is often stretched out into three syllables to become "smoo-ah-ooth." "Tire" is pronounced "tar"; barbed wire is "bob whar." L's are often completely left out, as in "he'p" for "help." An R is added to the end of a word wherever possible. Grandma's first name, the biblical and lovely "Leah," was pronounced "Lear."

If the old vernacular suited folks just fine, thank you very much, lots of newfangled words and expressions did not. Some words just coming into currency in my young days were considered too citified or pompous or silly to even be uttered. "Guys" meant effete city dudes; instead, men were called "fellers" (but never "fellas"). "Kids" were baby goats, and the word was not to be used to mean human "chillurn" or "young'uns."

While folks didn't always cotton to new words, their vocabularies included a whole string of "old" ones that the prim and proper — even today — would never let cross their lips. Profanity was frowned upon, but men did cuss and some women let loose with a "hell" or "damn" from time to time. Scatological and anatomical words were another matter. A tit was a tit, and folks called a fart a fart. People sometimes "passed gas" or "cut bullet patches," but I never heard the term "break wind" until I was almost grown. (The term "cutting bullet patches" dates back to the days of muzzle-loading firearms when bits of cloth were rammed down the gun barrel between the powder and the shot. Old underwear, whether cut up for the purpose or ripped apart by other purported means, served just fine.)

Folks from other climes have, in general, learned to tolerate — or at least keep quiet about — the funny way we talk. With one exception: many cannot understand why we grownups call our also grownup daddies "Daddy." They figure that it's like still talking baby talk after you've sprouted boobs or whiskers.

Our "grownup" use of the title "Daddy" goes back to the very early frontier and has lasted till now because the possible alternatives just don't fit. I suppose we could call our daddies "Dad," but that just hasn't sounded right in the past. Nowadays, some Piney Woods guys are called "Dad" by their kids. As more and more families become engrossed in Little League and soccer and Celtic dance lessons and Tae Kwan Do, that usage may become standard. But don't bet on it yet.

We could call our daddies "Father," but that very word denotes an Old World formality that, along with powdered wigs, the pioneers gladly left behind. Also, the word "Father" shouts out authority, as some mothers well know when they tell a misbehaving child, "just wait till your father gets home and hears about this." Many Piney Woods mamas would have simply whupped that young'un's butt and ended the whole shebang right then and there.

In the olden days, menfolks did usually manage the family's slim finances with an iron fist, and some could be tyrannical in other ways – even those called "Daddy" or "Pa" or "Papa." In general, though, they were not the lord and master of all they surveyed. This didn't necessarily leave the field open for women to run the whole show. There were some domineering women and also some mousy ones who allowed themselves to become indentured wives.

Back then, though, the two sexes usually respected one another. I sense it in the tales I've heard, and I used to see it first hand. Instead of being considered mentally inferior or weaklings, women were treated as responsible human beings. Men didn't have to be macho to prove their masculinity. I think calling them "Pa" or "Papa" or "Daddy" probably squelched any inklings in this direction.

If men and women respected and pretty much treated each other as equals, mutual respect also prevailed among men. In those days before the term "one-upmanship" had been coined, men didn't try to impress upon one another how smart or rich or important they were, maybe because everyone already knew everybody else's true circumstances anyway. Besides, bragging — by anybody — in those days was considered about as unmannerly as "cutting bullet patches" in church.

I suspect that scratching out a living under the frontier conditions that lasted so long in our neck of the woods had a lot to do with all the mutual respect amongst everybody. Men's masculinity and women's competence had to be drawn on day in and day out, and both could usually be taken for granted. Also, in a way of life such as this, cooperation is clearly more important than competition. (Note that those were the days before Texas — and a lot of the rest of the country — became obsessed with football.)

3
Dos and Don'ts

Today, when we think about the hardships that faced the pioneers, deaths from thirst and starvation usually come to mind, along with wagon trains becoming snowbound or even lost. River crossings, a far more frequent peril, did not get writ as large in our collective memory. Yet the pioneers had to somehow get their wagons, children, and livestock across many large rivers, especially on the eastern side of the continent. These rivers, then untamed by dams and levees, included the Tennessee, Arkansas, Red, and Missouri — and, of course, the Mississippi.

At some established crossings on the Pioneer Trails, local settlers made a few coins by winching "ferries" (essentially large homemade rafts) back and forth by muscle power. Often such trailblazing was yet to come. I heard how crossings were made in that situation from a really old man, who, in his younger days, had heard about it from his elders.

The pioneers caulked their wagons so they'd float, and they ran a husky rope across the river and snugged it down tightly on both sides. Then they'd unhitch their teams and swim all the livestock across. To get across in a floating wagon, they'd hang on to the rope with all their might while pulling on it to inch the wagon forward. Because the wet rope stretched and the current pushed against the wagon, they'd often reach the other shore a mile or so downstream from where they started.

Once upon a time a little girl aboard a floating wagon took off one of her shoes, leaned out over the river, and scooped up a drink of water in it. The little girl was my great-great grandmother; the year, about 1839. I heard the tale of the little girl who drank from her shoe many times during my younger years. She and her family were on their way to Texas, and though the tale never included the name of the river, I have decided that it must have been the Missouri. The story goes on to say that the little girl's mama spanked her for risking the only pair of shoes she would have that year.

Before they started on their trek, the little girl's parents may have laid down some dos and don'ts. If so, it would never, ever have entered their heads to include "don't drink from your shoe." I've heard mamas — and mothers — describe similar occurrences. That is, when they're sure they've covered all the dos and don'ts they can think of, some young'un will dream up something completely out of the blue.

Most parents in our bunch laid down few do-and-don't edicts. Maybe they knew we'd come up with something worse, or more outlandish, anyway. Besides, we young'uns instinctively knew most of what our families and society expected of us. We, and some of our adult kinfolks, didn't always "do or don't" what we were supposed to. And we sometimes, so to speak, "drank from our shoes."

No one ever told us to clean our plates, although we usually did because we served ourselves and took what we knew we wanted. Neither did anyone badger us about bathing or brushing our teeth; I guess we were clean enough though — considering that we'd bathed in a washtub. Folks seldom told us what to wear. We knew we had to look nice for school and church, but otherwise we wore whatever we wanted to as long as we didn't look indecent. One big no-no was to come to the table without first washing our hands; another was to go to bed with dirty feet.

Without being told, we knew we absolutely had to always tell the truth, make the best grades we could in school, never sass an adult, and respect other people's property. We did get spanked but it was almost always for being "aggervating," and especially for "aggervating" the grownups. When we really "aggervated" (or irritated, as we have now learned to say) an adult, we'd get our butt "whupped," usually by our mamas.

There were scads of taboos in the olden days that anyone coming of age since about the mid-1960s would find completely foreign and incomprehensible. There were, of course, all the sexual taboos, plus lots of others. Some had to do with religion and what the Bible says, or often with locally held views of what the Bible says. Also, superstitions that could be applied to just about any and everything abounded. In many cases, the boundary between religious and superstitious dictums had long vanished.

Society at large paid a lot more attention to all these dos and don'ts than most of our family ever did. Pregnancy out of wedlock was scandalous, but there were several bastards (in the illegitimate sense) in our family. This was not hushed up nor were the perpetrators or their children ostracized. Our family did keep quiet about one blatant case of almost pure bigamy, but everyone in the area knew about it anyway. Fornication was a sin, yet it was generally accepted as human nature that young folks were not always "virtuous." Divorce was also a sin, yet Daddy, and a few others had been divorced. Early on, my great grandmother's second husband didn't treat her right, so she ran him off and married a third time.

Also, the devout maintained that one was not supposed to go fishing on Sunday. To reinforce this taboo they frequently told about the man who went fishing on Sunday and caught a bona fide devil — complete with cloven hooves and a forked tail. We always went fishing whenever we could find the time, which was far too seldom.

Women were not supposed to smoke, but lots of them dipped snuff. And I don't mean little dainty sniffs from a decorated snuff bottle, but about a quarter-teaspoon's worth packed under the lower lip. Spittoons were prevalent, but more often women carried around an old tin can for the purpose.

Until World War II, women did *not* wear trousers, hence they had to ride sidesaddle (although I don't think anyone in our family ever owned a *real* sidesaddle). Women, except for me, pretty much abided by this restriction, and Grandma once preached to me that the Lord didn't like to see me astraddle a horse and, besides, God said in the Bible that "a woman in men's clothing is an abomination in My sight."

I don't know where the notion got started that grown men should not cry, but it certainly wasn't in our neck of the woods. I've seen men shed as many tears at funerals as women. Daddy cried when he heard that Will Rogers had been killed. Grandpa cried when his son Dale left for the army in World War II.

In spite of, or maybe because of, the shortage of do-and-don't edicts, our family has always gotten along together better than lots of other families. We've had our share of spats and a few family feuds and even a homicide, but in general we've laughed at life and poked fun at both the sacred and the profane. (This has often required some attitude adjustment on the part of newlywed inlaws who came from families with a more serious bent.)

I think we can credit a good bit of our family harmony to two of our basic unedicted "rules of order."

- We never — well, hardly ever — passed judgment on other people's way of life.
- We never — and even hardlier ever — gave unasked-for advice to anyone.

I could tell you that these are two good rules for peaceable living, but I won't since you haven't asked me for advice.

#1 Under the Black Gum Hog Hunting

Until about the 1950s, most of the land in the Piney Woods was officially open range. That is, no "leash law" decreed that livestock be kept behind fences, resulting in only a smidgen of the area being off limits to man or beast (or woman or child). So, besides supplying its inhabitants with wood for lumber, for the fireplace, for ax handles and such, the Piney Woods served them in many other ways. Folks picked berries for jelly and cobblers; they sometimes raided wild beehives for honey to go on their biscuits. Then, in the spring, big armloads of yellow jasmine and dogwood blossoms had to be brought in to brighten up the house.

With open range, folks didn't have to bother much with hay. In the olden days, almost no one had a barn. Instead they had cribs for storing corn to feed the milk cows, horses, mules, and chickens in the morning and at suppertime. Other than that, livestock were free to graze and forage in the woods. To keep all these animals from trampling around where they didn't belong, in the days before barbed wire, folks split rails and pickets from logs to fence in their yards, crops, and gardens.

This arrangement suited all involved. The cows, horses, and mules kept their domesticated instincts and usually came home at feeding time. The chickens stayed domesticated enough except in one respect. That is, given the opportunity, hens take diabolical pleasure in hiding their nests. Thus the daily egg-collecting chore included scouting around in the woods for hens' nests.

If hogs ever had even the slimmest iota of domesticity, they can slough it off in one oink. They would have been rooting around in the woods for "mast," that is, fallen acorns, berries, and such, all their lives and were as wild as what today is known as "feral pigs." So the men folks spent many and many a day riding all over the woods on horseback tracking down their family's hogs. This was called "hog hunting," but it had nothing to do with "hunting," as in "fox hunting" or "deer hunting."

One order of business on a hog hunt was to earmark the shoats (that is, the young pigs) so folks could always identify which hogs belonged to whom. Each family had its own registered earmark that consisted of a specific pattern of notches and squares snipped out of the end of the hog's ear. Some families also had a registered brand for their cattle, but hogs were always earmarked. (Branding a hog would have been about as easy as braiding a lion's tail.)

Young boars had to be "cut," a polite word for "castrate," so they would be fit for the table later. And a few hogs were taken home to be penned up and corn-fed for a supply of ham and sausage. Since there was no refrigeration in the olden days, hogs were butchered and the meat smoked during a cold spell, so people hunted hogs mostly in winter.

Men folks hog hunted mostly because it was essential to their way of life. But partly also, I think, because it was fun. It was a whole lot easier than plowing, but could also be dangerous. If it had been a good year for mast, the boars could weigh over 200 pounds and have "tushes," that is, tusks, four or more inches long. Once when Grandpa was hog hunting all by "his self," a big boar managed to knock him down, then locked its jaws around his arm. Just as the hog was about to grab Grandpa's throat, his dog jumped into the fray and fought the hog off.

The cancellation of the open range provision came as no surprise. The possibility had been bandied about for a good while before it became official. With so many of the young men serving in the military during World War II, then not returning to the farm, hog hunting had become the province of elderly men anyway, and it soon faded into the memories of bygone days.

The arts and skills and such of cowboys have long been glamorized in books and paintings and movies and our collective consciousness. Some Texas cities even have fancy statues of cowboys at work. A few old timers are still around who can recall the hog hunting days, and can even "read" an earmark. But there's nary a statue anywhere glamorizing a Piney Woodsian "cutting" an uncooperative male shoat.

4
THE EARLY SETTLERS: GRANDPA'S LINEAGE

Before Daddy (Fred Graham) married Mama he was what could be called an adult orphan. Born in Buffalo, New York, to Scottish immigrants, his family moved to Norfolk, Virginia, when he was too young to remember New York. By the time he finished high school in Norfolk at age 16, both his parents had died, and he struck out on his own. He had a knack for anything mechanical, so he had no trouble finding jobs as he wandered westward. He eventually reached San Francisco, where he went to college to study mechanical engineering. He then shifted his direction to eastward, later ending up in East Texas designing oil field pumping units.

If Daddy felt any pangs of kinfolks envy, marrying Mama cured them. Along with her small immediate family, instead of a dowry she presented him with 64 first cousins and no telling how many other cousins and aunts and uncles.

Mama (Lillian Russell) was born to Eli (Grandpa) and Leah Sowell Russell (Grandma) in Oak Flat. Besides the Russells, our lineage on Grandpa's side includes the Chestnuts. On Grandma's side, besides the Sowells it includes the Renfros and the Browns.

I've always shied away from genealogy. Just the thought of Mama's hordes of kinfolks has made it, to my way of thinking, as mind boggling a proposition as plotting out all the connections on the Internet. Two of my cousins have done a lot of genealogical research and kindly supplied me with details, which I've used as a road map for sorting out what I heard from the old timers. But I won't bother you with a bunch of begats. I'd rather tell about such things as what happened when Uncle Thedford's wife ran off and left him.

James Eason Russell

James Eason (1824-1903) and Caroline Welch Russell (1826-1894)

If someone in Oak Flat told you to go collect rocks in the wheelbarrow and not come back until it was full, you'd be gone a long time. But in the really olden days, if they had told you to fill it with petrified wood, you'd have gotten back sooner. When I was growing up we still occasionally ran across little chunks, but by then most of it had been found and taken away as souvenirs and such. There is still one magnificent specimen of it left from the early days though that any and all can go see. It forms the gravestone of James Eason Russell and his wife Caroline Welch Russell (Grandpa's grandparents).

James Eason and probably Caroline were born in Arkansas. It's my guess that they all lived somewhere around Russellville, Arkansas. By 1853, James Eason and Caroline were married and had at least one offspring, my Great-Grandpa Bill (Grandpa's daddy). In that year James Eason packed up his family, which may have included some inlaws, and set out for Texas. It would have taken them at least a month to get to the Piney Woods, a distance I reckon at about 500 miles.

Nine months later, James Eason got homesick for Arkansas and packed up the family again and moved back. Once there though, he found that he missed the tall pines and streams of the Piney Woods more than he had missed the hills of Arkansas. So back they went to what is now Angelina County, where he and Caroline lived out the rest of their lives.

Along about this time, one inlaw, Caroline's sister (I don't know her name.), had begun to figure prominently in the family's affairs. She lived within traveling distance of James Eason and Caroline, but not just right down the road, and (at least later) had a family of her own.

I heard the story of James Eason and his family first from Mama when I was a know-it-all teenager. It was election year and "speakins" were being held anywhere and anytime the candidates could find an audience. The annual graveyard workin' was coming up, when everybody took hoes, rakes, and a basket dinner (for noontime) and spent the day weeding the cemetery, repairing gravestones, and doing a lot of eating, singing, and socializing. Graveyard workins always drew a big crowd and, in an election year, a speakin' was included for the candidates.

Two upstanding citizens were running for County Commissioner, then and now an important county office. One candidate was a cousin of ours, the other a long-time family friend. It was a tight race and I wondered how our family would decide which one to vote for. A few days before the graveyard workin' I thought I had it figured out. So I commented to Mama, in what I took to be a very sophisticated adult way, that our relatives wouldn't have to ponder the race because they'd just naturally vote for our cousin. Mama answered sharply enough to put me in my place, but quietly enough for me to know she was about to let me in on a big secret.

And that is, that James Eason sired two families. When Caroline would get pregnant, her sister would come stay to help with the delivery and recuperation. By the time for the sister to go back to her own home, she would be pregnant.

I don't know what the sister's husband thought, or if she even had one. The bar sinister children did not take on the name of Russell, but rather kept their mother's family name (Welch). And, the whole affair was not a big secret. It was, and to some extent still is, common knowledge around the community. But we never talked about it except around close kinfolks.

Mama also told me that our cousin's opponent in the Commissioner's race was kin to us on the sister's side, and both candidates were "the same amount of kinfolks" to us. I think that's why Mama told me about it when she did. She didn't want me blabbing off something ignorant and embarrassing about "kinfolks" at the graveyard working.

A few folks have asked if James Eason was Mormon, but I'm almost certain he wasn't. During that period the Mormons had their hands full migrating from New York state and getting established in Utah and were almost unheard of in Texas. Besides, Mormons don't even drink coffee, and it's been said that, in a saloon brawl, James Eason got shot in the arm, which dangled limply thereafter (apparently the only part of him that did).

James Eason probably learned to question conventionality early on. His daddy, George Russell, was Davy Crockett's sidekick who fought with him in the Cherokee wars in Tennessee and went with him to Washington when Davy was in Congress. (He didn't go with him to the Alamo.) I'd bet James Eason heard, probably more than once, Davy's motto: "Be sure you're right, then go ahead."

James Eason surely must have thought about his conjugal arrangement and maybe recalled the motto. At any rate, he and both sisters apparently had no qualms about their way of life. From what I've heard, the two halves of the family got along together pretty good. My Great Uncle "Dock," James Eason's and Caroline's son, said they all considered one another as part of one big family with no partiality shown in either direction. But, to me, the cemetery plot of James Eason and Caroline speaks louder than words about their unconventional family.

In the olden days, putting a proper tombstone on relatives' graves was about like painting a house. Most people couldn't afford it, but it was something they'd like to get around to someday. Hence, a lot of old hand-carved, bare wood grave markers deteriorated and crumbled with age (just like a lot of the older unpainted houses). It was a mark of respect and devotion — and also prosperity —when a family placed some kind of permanent marker on a grave.

The gravestone on James Eason's and Caroline's grave is about as permanent as a marker can be, and it's the most prominent one in the cemetery. One day when Uncle Dock was out in the woods, he found the petrified log and got a man by the name of Weed Wilson to haul it on his two-wheeled log cart to the cemetery. It's a good-sized log that, before it petrified, would have yielded a heap of nice wooden planks.

It lies flat and is long enough to span the head of James Eason's and Caroline's graves. Throughout the cemetery, many other markers bear the names of the Russells and their descendants. In the rows adjoining one side of James Eason's and Caroline's graves, the markers are inscribed with the name of Welch.

PETRIFIED GRAVE STONE OF JAMES EASON AND CAROLINE WELCH

WILLIAM D. RUSSELL ("GRANDPA BILL"), 2/18/1848–4/16/1942:

Grandpa Bill, Grandpa's daddy, lived in the Piney Woods for almost all of his 94 years. He was 13 when the Civil War started, and he died toward the end of World War II. The local Indians were not consigned to a reservation until well into his middle years. During his old age, when an airplane occasionally flew over, everyone ran out to get a glimpse of it. Tracks for scheduled rail service were built in East Texas in the 1880s, but before that, Grandpa Bill took the only train ride of his life on a flat car meant for hauling cotton bales.

GRANDPA BILL RUSSELL IN HIS EARLY 90S ON HIS FRONT STEPS (CIRCA 1940)

Historians tell us that during the Civil War (1861–1865), very few young men were to be found in East Texas because most of them had gone off to fight the Yankees. Grandpa Bill joined their ranks in the autumn of 1864, when he was 17 (He might have been drafted.). He and some other Piney Woods boys were assigned to Col. Bauder's regiment in Galveston. I don't know when, if ever, he got a gray army uniform; maybe never at that late stage of the war. I do know that he bought a brand new hat for the adventure. By autumn the cotton crop would have been sold, that is, if it could have been during the wartime era, and the family might have had a few Confederate dollars to pass around. At any rate, he was mighty proud of that hat.

Together with some other boys from the area, he was loaded onto a railroad flatcar for the trip to Galveston, a distance of about 150 miles.

Somewhere along the way a wind came up, and together with the speed of the train — probably all of 20 miles per hour — his hat blew off and flew away. So before he ever got out of the Piney Woods and reached the Texas Gulf coast plains, he had lost his prized hat.

The rest of his tour of duty wasn't even that eventful. Shortly before he left on the flat car there had been a skirmish in Galveston between Union and Confederate forces, and all the residents got scared and left. He said the city was deserted, with lots of vacant houses. Seven months later, the Confederacy surrendered and its soldiers discharged at wherever spot they happened to be. So Grandpa Bill and the other Piney Woods boys had to get back home on their own.

An epidemic of dysentery had made the rounds of the army camp just before he was discharged. So, in addition to having to walk back to Angelina County, he and his buddies were laid low with all the miseries of that malady. They were some better by the time they reached the Piney Woods, but weak from starvation. Then they came upon a clearing in the woods where some cows with calves were grazing. Being farm boys, they knew that cows with calves give milk. They found the house nearby, explained their situation to the farmwife, and asked if she could spare some milk. She answered, "You boys can have all the milk you want," then told them to come in and sit down. She cooked them up a big pone of cornbread to go with the milk. Thus fortified, they found their way on home.

When Grandpa Bill got home, he didn't waste much time getting married and starting a family. Within four years, he had married Mary Chestnut and they had Uncle Jimmy, their first child. During the following 22 years (through 1891) they had nine more children.

Except for some typical crimes and misdemeanors here and there by individuals, life has always been reasonably peaceful in the Piney Woods. Indians did live in and roam freely in the area, but the bloody conflicts in Texas occurred farther to the west. The Piney Woodsians distrusted the Indians, and vice versa, but they kept the peace by avoiding one another. One day, though, when Grandpa Bill was a young man and out in the woods, he came upon an encampment of Indians. They were roasting venison over a campfire, and Grandpa Bill would rather have skedaddled, but when they invited him to sit down and eat, he figured he'd better do it. They handed him a chunk of meat that had a lot of little white round things on it that he thought was rice. When he began to eat, he realized that the little things were maggots. He didn't dare not eat, so he pretended to chew. Every chance he got, he tore off hunks of the meat and slipped them to the dogs. After he "finished eating," he told the Indians goodbye, and skedaddled away.

Grandpa Bill worked his boys (Jimmy, Thedford, and Grandpa) hard, but they took it as a fact of life and got even by kidding him. Once, as they told it, Grandpa Bill was out in the cow-pen along about dusky dark helping with the milking. (If you've never been in a cow-pen at dusky dark, you'll have to use your imagination, and also judge for yourself whether the tale is true.) A breeze came up and, once again, blew off Grandpa Bill's hat. His boys said he had to try on three before he found the right one!

I don't think Grandpa Bill took the kidding by his boys seriously. The only time I know of that he got mad was when he lost his temper because a stubborn cow wouldn't go where he wanted her to go. He was so mad he gave her a mighty whack over the head with his cane. I still have that cane, complete with the wire wrapping holding it's upper and lower parts together where it broke when it hit the cow's head. Hand-carved from a stout limb of hickory by an ex-slave in Alabama, the cane has an inscription that says, "Jesus, Walk With Me Today." Uncle Bud had it made when he was on a lumbering job in Alabama and gave it to Grandpa Bill.

Grandpa Bill outlived Grandma Mary Chestnut by 29 years and spent about the first half of those years as a widower. Along about then he decided he'd been single long enough and married Mattie. In our family we called her "Aunt" Mattie to imply that she was not to be confused with or compared to Grandma Mary Chestnut, but everyone knew she was a "good woman and a hard worker," about one of the highest compliments a woman could get in the Piney Woods.

As the story goes, Aunt Mattie was living with some of her kinfolks a few miles away from Grandpa Bill's place. He went over on horseback to see her, and when he rode up she came out to the front gate to greet him.

After a few "howdy-dos," he said, while still on his horse, "Mattie, I'm looking to get married."

She replied, "Well, I'm looking to get married too."

Then Grandpa Bill told her, "All right. I'll come over in the wagon next Saturday to get you and your things."

And that's what happened. They did get officially married, and Aunt Mattie lived with Grandpa Bill until the end of his long life. She was a good wife and, after a stroke paralyzed him along about 1930, a good caretaker.

I was nine when Grandpa Bill died, and I visited him and Aunt Mattie a lot in his later years. His eyesight had pretty much failed, and he couldn't get around because of the stroke, but his mind was still sharp. He sat in a chair by the fireplace in the winter and on the front porch in summer. I'd climb up into his lap, and he'd say, "Now which young'un are you?" and someone would tell him "That's Winiferd" (as they pronounced it). And he'd say "All right," and smile. He smoked a pipe as continuously as possible and smelled of tobacco and the homemade lye soap everyone used. I remember that we talked, but I don't recall about what. I do remember his cheerful smile and chuckle. As I look back on it, the feeling that comes back to me is that he was serene and content.

Mary Chestnut Russell 7/10/1852–7/4/1913:

According to Mama, the Chestnuts settled first in America in the Carolinas and had a lot of French blood. My guess from this is that they were Huguenots. History tells us that the Huguenots were French Protestants caught up in what today we would call "ethnic cleansing" during the religious wars in France in the fifteen and sixteen hundreds. Many were slain; some fled to Germany, others to England. Later a batch of them from England went to the Carolinas and established a colony under British rule. Whether our Chestnut line was part of all this or not, they eventually got to Texas and started a large family of Piney Woodsians that included Grandma Mary Chestnut (Grandpa's mama).

From what I've been told, I believe we get some of our best traits from Grandma Mary Chestnut. Most of our predecessors had a good sense of humor, that is, a knack for laughing at the world's silliness. According to Mama though, our wit, that is, our knack for saying funny things to show how silly the world really is, came to us from Grandma Mary Chestnut.

Also, many of the Russells from Grandpa's generation on are avid gardeners (one of the very best traits a person can have). I think this love of flowers came from Grandma Mary Chestnut. One day Grandpa sent one of his girls on an errand to Grandma Mary Chestnut. As the young girl was leaving to go back home, Grandma Mary Chestnut went out and picked a rose and said, "Today is Eli's birthday. You take him this rose, and be sure to tell him it's for his birthday."

Grandpa Eli rooted that rose, then planted it out in the middle of the cornfield, where it grew and flourished. For many years afterwards, whoever plowed that field had to make a big circle around the rose bush so it wouldn't get damaged.

From all I've heard, Grandma Mary Chestnut must have been a thoughtful and considerate person, and a story Aunt Addie (Grandpa's sister) told me points up how mindful of her children Grandma Mary Chestnut was.

Aunt Addie said that long ago her mama told her, "Now Addie, if anything happens to me, I want you to look out for my boys. I don't worry too much about you girls. You'll be all right. Who I worry about most is Jimmy."

But Grandma Mary Chestnut could also be firm. When Grandpa was a young boy, she once "whupped" his butt for being "aggervatin." She had been spinning yarn, and there was always an unusable but long piece that came off the spinning wheel first, which was given to the young uns' to make playthings with. Grandpa said he took the one she gave him and made a lasso out of it. He was sitting on the front porch when a rooster walked by. He tried to rope it but missed. The rooster jumped away squawking. A few minutes later he got another chance, but missed again. He tried several times, and kept missing, with the rooster raising a hullabaloo each time.

Finally Grandma Mary Chestnut came out of the house and told him to quit or she'd "whup" him. She went back inside, and a few minutes later the rooster walked by again. Grandpa said he couldn't resist just one last try. This time he did lasso the rooster, and it raised holy hell. His mama came tearing out of the house and "whupped" him good and proper.

Grandma Mary Chestnut lived to be 61. She was apparently in good health so her death came as a surprise. The family had just finished eating breakfast when she got up from the table, went into another room, and collapsed and died. Her heart might have given out; Mama said that she had long been troubled with angina. But by then, all of her children were in their late teens or older, and Uncle Jimmy was 44.

#2 UNDER THE BLACK GUM
HOW UNCLE BUD GOT HIS NAME

If you're the ninth young'un to come along, you can figure that the ones before you have used up your parents' knack (and enthusiasm) for picking out names. So when Grandpa Bill's and Grandma Mary Chestnut's ninth baby came along, they just called him "Bud." He got a more official name later, but for all his 86 years he was known to almost everybody as just plain Bud.

Uncle Bud worked at logging jobs in the Piney Woods as a teenager, and later at various places in the Southern timber belt as a lumber inspector. Throughout World War II, he worked for the Southern Pine Association in Washington, D.C., then took a job in Honduras with a mahogany logging and milling company. In the mid 1950s he and his wife moved back to Oak Flat where they built a brick house and lived out their slightly over 20 years of retirement.

When it came time for Uncle Bud to register for first grade, his folks decided he needed a better name on his school records than Bud. They also decided that he was old enough to choose his own name.

After he'd thought about it a while, Uncle Bud told them he might like to be named after Horace Greeley, the New York newspaper editor who had lobbied for farm folks and popularized the term, "Go West, young man." So he said to Grandma Mary Chestnut, "Mama, I'll go hide behind a bush in the yard and you holler out 'Horace' like you're calling me to dinner and we'll see how it sounds."

Uncle Bud hid, and Grandma Chestnut hollered. After only one "Horrrraccess", he jumped up from behind the bush, screaming at the top of his lungs, "That's a terrible name, don't you ever call me that again."

The name they settled on came from who knows where. Officially he was Earl Jackson Russell. Some of his casual acquaintances or coworkers might have called him Earl or even E.J. But no one in the family ever called him to the table by any name other than Bud.

5
The Early Settlers: Grandma's Lineage

The early settlers in Grandma's line (the Renfros and the Browns) arrived in the Piney Woods shortly after Texas won its independence from Mexico. Within a few years they were well established. Some of them, and their progeny, never achieved much in the way of fame and fortune. Others became prominent in the community and even lived in painted houses.

The Renfros

Our family history in the Renfro line dates back to 1797. In that year Napoleon was carrying on in Europe and John Adams was inaugurated as the second president of the United States. John Folkner Renfro was also born that year in Kentucky.

By 1800, Thomas Jefferson had become the third president. Napoleon was still carrying on in Europe. Firearms were muzzle loading, that is, the kind where powder from a powder horn, the wadding (sometimes "bullet patches"), and the ball or shot are shoved down the business end of the gun barrel with a ramrod.

In 1809, James Madison became the fourth president. Napoleon, still carrying on in Europe, divorced Josephine. Abraham Lincoln was born in Kentucky, and so was Rebecca Harrison Hicks.

By the mid-1820s, John F. and Rebecca had married and lived in Missouri. At least four of their many offspring were born there, including, in 1838, Margarette Lucinda, whom we call "Granny Hutch." The very next year John F. packed up his family and wagons and moved to Texas. After living a short while in Sabine County, they settled in Angelina County on what became known as Renfro Prairie.

Texas became an independent nation in 1836; thus, when John F. and his family moved from Missouri, they were actually leaving the United States. Texas laws and its Constitution were almost carbon copies of those of the U.S., but otherwise Texas was a do-it-yourself place where everything had to be started from scratch. This, of course, included schools. So early on, John F. built one of the first public schools in Angelina County on his land at Renfro Prairie. Over fifty years later the school was still going strong, with an 1895 report showing 24 students at the Renfro Prairie School. I suspect that a lot of the students were Renfros since John F. and Rebecca did have a batch of young'uns and grand-young'uns.

Some of their progeny migrated to faraway places like Mobile, Alabama; others stayed closer to home. Several of their children died young, including four sons who died while in the Confederate Army — from illness, I think, rather than from battle. One of their sons, Isaac P. Renfro, however, came through three wars unscathed.

Born in Missouri in 1829, according to one record Isaac P. lived to the ripe old age of 99. At the age of ten (the year the family settled in Texas), he became a teamster in General Taylor's army. At 17 he enlisted during the U.S. –Mexican War (when Mexico had gotten really riled up over the U.S. annexing Texas, California and parts between). He was about 35 when he enlisted as a teamster in the Confederate Army. It's not clear that Isaac P. lived to 99, but he certainly didn't die young; I guess the soldier's life agreed with him.

Somewhere in between all of his soldiering, Isaac P. and his wife Sarah Ainsworth had a whole batch of young'uns, with at least one son becoming prominent in the county. Isaac P. named this son after his own father, so I'll refer to him as John F. 2 to avoid confusion.

John F. 2 was born in 1866, a little over a year after his Daddy got home from the Civil War. As a young adult he settled in Huntington and lived there the rest of his life. His first wife, Allie Sayers, died young, probably in childbirth. He later remarried, and his second wife, Arkansas Hawkins, outlived him by several years. At age 33, in 1899, John F. 2 graduated from Sam Houston Normal College, now known as Sam Houston State University, in Huntsville (where Mama went about 20 years later). It would have been unusual in those days for a 33-year-old married man to attend and graduate from college, but then John F. 2 did lead a busy life.

The year after he graduated, he followed in the footsteps of his granddaddy and started Huntington's first school on his property in town where it stayed for 13 years until new school buildings were built on another site.

Over the years John F. 2 was a school trustee, owned several thousand acres of timber and grazing land, and was an ordained minister although he never pastored a church. He organized Huntington's first bank and served on its board, but the bank didn't make it very far in the Depression. In his early years he served three years in the State Legislature.

Judging by John F. 2's record, he was what today we'd call a compulsive workaholic. Way back, when Grandma did something that "aggervated" Grandpa, he'd tell her, "That'll be the Renfro there are in you". (I don't think the Russells' rambunctious ways meshed with the more serious Renfro ways.) Anyhow, those of us today who are compulsive workaholics can just say, "That'll be the Renfro there are in me."

The Browns

Grandma's great-grandparents on the Brown side settled in what later became San Augustine County, an area that already had a long history when the Browns and other settlers from the United States got there.

By the mid-1500s, about 50 years after Columbus discovered America, Spanish explorers were traipsing around, and getting lost, in "Texas." By the 1700s, Spain had claimed all of what is now the U.S. Southwest, and was doing its best to send over enough soldiers and priests to civilize the place. It built roads, that is, wagon trails that were established and identifiable so travelers could get from one place to another without getting lost.

The major roads, called the King's Highway (El Camino Real), include one now known as The Old San Antonio Road. It connected Spanish outposts and settlements in what's now Louisiana to, obviously, San Antonio. Its paved version still runs from Natchitoches, Louisiana, through Nacogdoches, Texas (two places radio and TV announcers persistently confuse and mispronounce every time anything newsworthy happens at either place). In 1717 the Spanish built a mission they named Mission Delores de los Ais in between these two towns where the city of San Augustine is now.

"Ais" translates into "mean Indian," which is what one band of local troublesome Indians was called by the other Indian tribes and the Spaniards. The mission was active for at least 50 years. But by then the "mean Indians" must have been subdued or pacified or something, because the mission was left to tumble down and disappear.

Mexico, which then included what's now the U.S. Southwest, gained its independence from Spain in 1813. Early on during the Mexican period, a settlement around what was by then the "old mission" grew and became known as San Augustine. In the 1820s "Americans" began settling in the area under the terms of Stephen Austin's agreement with Mexico (which meant the settlers had to become Catholic).

Right after Texas gained independence from Mexico and became a Republic, its Congress got busy establishing counties and county seats. One of the first was San Augustine County, with the town of San Augustine as the county seat. But American settlers coming to the area during that period called it Ayish Bayou (probably, I'd bet, because they didn't want to live in a place that sounded so Catholic and Hispanic). So when our Brown ancestors migrated there during the days of the Republic of Texas, they settled on what the "Texians" preferred to call the Ayish Bayou.

Our founding ancestors in this line were Richard O. Brown (1805-1875) and his wife, Nancy Baumgartner (1810-1895). Richard was born in Tennessee, Nancy in Virginia (how Richard and Nancy found one another and got married will have to remain one of life's minor mysteries). They lived in Tennessee for a few years then migrated to Mississippi. About three years later, in 1839, they moved to Texas. Two of their six children, including Grandma's grandpa John E. Brown, were born in Tennessee, one in Mississippi, and three in Texas. All the moving and childbearing doesn't seem to have affected Nancy's health. She outlived Richard by 20 years and died at age 85. Census data show that at age 70 she was head of a household in Nacogdoches County with three laborers and a grandson living with her.

Richard is always identified as Dr. R.O. Brown. We don't know if he was a bona fide doctor or some kind of blood-letter or bonesetter. He seems to have also been a farmer. His family did indeed live on their farm on the Ayish Bayou in an area then known as the Tennessee Settlement.

Two brothers, Jim and Levi Crow, also from Tennessee, lived right across the bayou from the Browns. Levi died right after he stepped on a rattlesnake and was bitten. Jim Crow married Richard and Nancy's daughter, Susan.

When it came time for the children of the Browns and the Crows to get out on their own, several moved down the road a piece to a new settlement called Smyrna (and pronounced "Smernie). Quite a few others settled there also, and, for over three generations, "Smernie" was a thriving, cotton-farming community.

In the early 1900s, folks began moving away, and in a few years "Smernie" had just dried up. Various reasons have been proposed for the exodus, one being that the area was prone to illnesses. Maybe. The measles caused many deaths in those days. (Richard's and Nancy's son

Richard, Jr., died of the measles while in the Confederate Army). Malaria was also common. (When I was a child in Lufkin, I came down with malaria.) Nevertheless, many Piney Woodsians had fond recollections of "Smernie." For nearly a century, folks with strong ties — and even not so strong ties — flocked to its annual homecoming. Grandma went to them religiously. The yearly event was to her what the Super Bowl is to today's sports fans.

Grandma was born in "Smernie," but her ties to it go back even further. Both her parents were born there (Grandma "Wade" and Pat Sowell); her Grandpa John E. Brown and his wife (Granny Hutch Renfro) settled there. Grandma once showed me a newspaper clipping listing the names of dozens of "Smernie" residents. She said, "I knew all these families, and most of them were my kinfolks." I knew only some of them, but one that stands out in my mind is Susan Brown, who married Jim Crow. (She will make another appearance in these pages later on.) She lived to a ripe old age, and I recall folks remembering her in more or less one word as "OldSusanBrownCrow."

6

GRANNY HUTCH AND HER TWO HUSBANDS: JOHN E. BROWN AND AARON HUTCHINSON

Margarette Lucinda Renfro (Granny Hutch) and John E. Brown got married on the 4th of July, 1858. About ten years later she married Aaron Hutchinson. Except for some tidbits in two letters John E. wrote to Granny Hutch and another to his parents while he was in the Confederate Army, we know nothing about those intervening years. And therein lie some mysteries.

In his letters, he brings up "Little Molly" several times. In one he asks Granny Hutch to "kiss Little Molly's sweet lips for me." In another he asks her to give Little Molly a good education if he doesn't return from the war. John E. left for the Army in 1862, so if Little Molly was his and Granny Hutch's daughter, as we've always assumed, she would have been about two or three years old when he wrote the letters. But Granny Hutch could have been raising a niece or, if John E. had been married previously, a child by a wife about whom we likewise know nothing. Besides what's in the letters there is no record, remembrance, or even a hint of Little Molly. We think she died and was buried privately around the time John E. wrote the letters. That would not have been unheard of in those days.

Grandpa Eli told of going to the Jonesville Cemetery for some reason back in the olden days, and finding a family there, all by "theirselves," quietly burying a child. He asked them why they didn't let folks know so neighbors could have helped dig the grave and hold a service.

They answered, "We didn't want to bother nobody. We've had so many die that folks have helped with, that we didn't want to put them to any trouble again."

At any rate, little Molly just disappeared, much as John E. was also to do.

Granny Hutch gave birth to Catherine Elizabeth (Grandma's mama and our "Grandma Wade") in April, 1863. We don't know whether John E. ever saw his new child, or even ever knew that Granny Hutch was pregnant. In fact, we don't know another thing about John E. Brown.

A YOUNG JOHN E. BROWN IN CONFEDERATE JACKET FROM A
WATCH-POCKET-SIZED TIN-TYPE

Enter Aaron Hutchinson. Aaron (sometimes spelled Aron) was born about 1837 in Derbyshire, England, and got married there in 1853. His wife died or he ran off and left her, because the next thing we know is that in October of 1861 he enlisted in the Confederate Army (Company D, 7th Texas Cavalry). Based on his wartime record, he probably wished many a time that he was back in England unless his life there had been utterly miserable.

In 1862, the year after the Civil War began, the Yanks took New Orleans in order to seal off the Mississippi River to Confederate seagoing traffic from the Gulf of Mexico. They then battled their way up the Mississippi corridor and captured Vicksburg the next year.

(A side note on this is that General Hooker, the Union Commander of occupied New Orleans, issued an edict to his troops to consider any female found out on the streets of New Orleans after dark a prostitute. The women who risked venturing out after curfew became known as "Hooker's Ladies," and legend has it that this is why prostitutes are now called "hookers.")

Now back to Aaron. In June of 1863 he was taken prisoner at Donaldsonville, which is on the Mississippi River about halfway between New Orleans and Baton Rouge. He was later paroled at New Orleans (because he was English?), then turned around and got captured again in July 1864, this time near the Louisiana–Arkansas border. The Yanks must have figured they didn't want him loose again, because the next thing we know is that in June of 1865, three months after the war ended, he was released from prison at Elmira, way off in upstate New York.

Within three years of his release he had made his way to the Piney Woods and married Granny Hutch. They had a very long life together. If they had any offspring, they didn't make it very long because Grandma Wade was Granny Hutch's only surviving child. Aaron died in 1912 of what was recorded as "cerebral softening." Granny Hutch lived another 13 years.

AARON HUTCHISON; GRANNY HUTCH'S SECOND HUSBAND

Now Granny Hutch wouldn't have married Aaron if John E. had still been around. But no one can find "John Brown's body." Kinfolks who have searched the Internet and Civil War records have found some intriguing clues, but again, nothing specifically on a John E. Brown from Texas. Also, family members who might have known about his fate are all long gone. But the lack of facts doesn't keep us from dreaming up various scenarios. You can decide which makes the most sense.

He could have been killed or died of pneumonia or something in the "Indian Nation" (Oklahoma), and is buried there. In one letter he writes: "We expect to start to the Indian Nation next Monday. We will go to Fort Gipson, which is two hundred miles from here."

Two pitched battles between about 3,000 Union soldiers, and over 1,500 Confederates were fought near Fort Gipson in July of 1863, with each side trying to gain control "of the frontier." The Union forces won big time, with an estimated 700 or so Confederate casualties.

It is also possible that John E. simply "disappeared." In his first letter he wrote, "I think I never will desert while I am treated right."
In his next letter he says, "...but (with) the Colonel and Lt. Colonel there is a heap (of) dissatisfaction...." If he did desert, he could have been caught and executed. Or he could have died or disappeared somewhere along the way in an attempt to either get back to East Texas or to some neutral territory such as Missouri.

My genealogically inclined kinfolks think, and I agree, that he became part of what was called "Terry's Texas Rangers." They had no connection to *the* widely known Texas Rangers; rather, they were called "rangers" because they ranged far and wide, sometimes miles behind enemy lines, to raid Union supply sources and generally make things miserable for the Feds. They fought in Kentucky, Tennessee (including Shiloh), and at Chickamauga (Georgia). And their tie to Fort Gibson in the Indian Nation looks fairly certain.

Terry's Texas Rangers started out as a regiment of 1,000 or so men mustered in at Houston and led by Benjamin Franklin Terry, a wealthy sugar planter from Brazoria. During the war, replacements, additional enlistees, and men transferring from other commands changed the makeup of the regiment, including its leadership. (Among others, Terry was killed in battle.)

Due to the wide-ranging exploits of Terry's Texas Rangers, and the comings and goings within their ranks, accurate and complete records are pretty scarce. (The professional genealogists point this out just about every chance they get.) So while we don't have official records, we've got some good clues.

In John E's second letter to Granny Hutch from "Bouey" County (Bowie?), the address he gives includes "Lane's Regiment…Texas Partes (partisans) and Rangers." In his letter to his parents he writes, "Colonel Lane has 12 companies in his regiment."

Terry's Texas Rangers fought in a bunch of skirmishes and battles in Tennessee in October 1863. They fared pretty well for a while but were later beaten almost to smithereens. After this defeat, those still able to travel scooted back to the relative safety of Northern Alabama. The chaplain of Terry's Texas Rangers, who was there, wrote a day-by-day account of this whole episode. Among the officers killed, he lists a John Martin Lane who just *might* be the above Colonel Lane. He also states, "We left in Tennessee at least 1,000 men. One half are doubtless killed, wounded, or taken prisoner."

One family genealogist did turn up a J. F. Brown in a roster of Terry's Texas Rangers. Now it doesn't seem farfetched that the bottom of the "E" somehow got pruned back to an "F." The only other thing we know about a J. F. Brown is that he was in prison in Elmira, N.Y.

To thicken the plot, let's imagine that John E. (or F) and Aaron got to know each other while in prison. Then let's say that John died and, when the war was over, Aaron made his way to East Texas to tell Granny Hutch what had happened to John. Maybe they fell madly in love and got married, or maybe they just both needed a companion.

Imaginations aside, they must have lived happily ever after, although I'd bet that took a lot of adjustment for a pioneer Texas woman and an Englishman. After Aaron died, Granny Hutch applied for and got a Confederate Widow's pension based on Aaron's war record. It probably came to less than ten dollars per month.

#3 Under the Black Gum
A Bone Felon Tale

Mama told a tale about one of our grandmothers, almost certainly Granny Hutch, who had a bone felon on her finger. I don't think anybody gets felons anymore but, like boils, they used to be common. The dictionary defines "felon" as a deep inflammation of the finger or toe.

The bone felon wouldn't heal and started spreading up Granny Hutch's finger into the palm of her hand. None of the remedies anybody tried, nor even a doctor's treatments, did any good, and the felon just kept spreading. It finally spread way up into her arm, making her helpless and miserable. The time then came when it seemed she wouldn't make it through another night. Everybody was so sure of this that the menfolks went out and got busy building her a coffin.

About that time a stranger on his way somewhere stopped at their house. When they told him what was going on, he said, "Why, I can heal that." He then went out on a big round in the woods and came back with a batch of leaves, roots, and bark. (The tale doesn't tell us what kind of plants these came from.) He made hot poultices out of them and had everybody apply them to her arm all through the night. By the next morning Granny Hutch was in fine shape. The men then took the coffin they had built up to the attic, and the family stored quilt scraps in it!

7
That Old-Time Religion

Grandma fixed an early supper of pancakes on the little three-burner coal oil (kerosene) stove. It was summertime and too hot to fire up the big wood stove except in the cool of the morning for breakfast, or for dinner — at noon — when only the big stove's cook-top could accommodate all the simmering pots. The pancakes weren't the little old thin, sissified plops now in fashion, but rather as big around as a dinner plate. A young'un usually couldn't eat but one, especially since we smothered them in cane "surp." After we'd finished eating and put on clean clothes, but not our "Sunday-go-to-meetin' duds," we left for church. It was not Sunday, but a traveling preacher in the area was holding services that night.

The church house was over a mile away, which in good weather we always walked (in bad weather we usually just skipped church, as did almost everyone else). Although it would still be daylight for a couple of hours, Grandma carried an unlit coal oil lamp since it would be well after dark before the preacher said his last amen. When we got to the church house, Grandma and the other women who had brought lamps set them on the pulpit, the piano, and here and there on window sills, ready to light when it got dark.

The church house had only one room. It was on the large size for a room but considerably small for a church sanctuary. Even so, the coal oil lamps didn't light it much more than a bright moon would have, and they cast flickering shadows on all the walls. Our neighbor Stella (pronounced "Steller") always brought her Aladdin lamp, which illuminated not from a burning wick but from a glowing mantle, and put out as much light as a small electric bulb. Stella and her son J. N. lived at least three miles from the church house though and often couldn't manage that long a walk.

The singing always came first and went on until all the old favorite hymns had been sung. Instead of a formal, organized choir that met regularly to rehearse, what was referred to as "the choir" consisted of those who wanted to sing. They would gather around the piano, even when nobody was there who could play the piano, for what in effect was an informal gospel jam session. The "saved people" on the front benches were usually the ones who went up to sing. People in the back pews either listened to the singing or talked quietly amongst themselves. I always sat toward the back of the church with my friends, but sometimes I would go up and sing. If our neighbor Floyd was there with his big acoustic guitar though, I always sat back to listen because he played, and also sang, just like Eddy Arnold.

The sermon came next and usually fell into one, or more, of several categories, each apparently regarded as a sure-fire way to prod sinners into salvation. There was the occasional gentle-persuasion one, when the preacher would speak in soft, pleading tones to explain how much Jesus loves everyone, even the sinner. But our country preachers then seemed to have the notion (as some preachers do now) that if they weren't yelling, they weren't preaching.

So they would blast off into another topic, often one aimed strictly at scaring the sinner into repentance. The preachers who favored this approach could depict in gory detail the hideous demons in hell and the four horsemen of the apocalypse and such. The flickering shadows in the church house added a dramatic touch. During these "scary sermons" I was always glad when Stella was there with her Aladdin lamp.

A favorite sermon topic of some preachers, though, dwelled long and often loud on the "ways" of sinners, which could include dancing, drinking, and cursing, right down to women wearing lipstick. Some of the "ways" of sinners did not involve sins at all, or maybe just little sins, but they could put you smack on the road to perdition. I vividly remember the warning that "a whistling woman and a crowing hen shall both wind up with some bad end" (and I quote verbatim).

I knew the preacher's goal was to save sinners, and with so many ways of sinning, probably everybody from the middle pews on back was guilty of one or more of them. But those people were my friends and kinfolks, and I knew of only a very few who'd ever done anything really wrong. Maybe the preacher knew of a "secret sinner" in the congregation, and was trying to flush him or her out.

In those days before the shenanigans of TV preachers, all the preachers I knew or knew of were honest, sincere, and staunch believers in what they preached. And, they were all poor. Some didn't have much education, and some were not "real bright," but they all meant well. They got no salary; rather, the collection — taken in a real hat — was given to them. Most people dropped in a few nickels or maybe a quarter. One or two of the men in the congregation might each deposit a dollar bill. Even in those pre-inflation days it didn't amount to an "income," and all of the country preachers had full-time jobs as loggers, farmers, carpenters, and such. Whatever they earned from preaching was just about enough to buy their children their yearly pair of shoes.

Even today when I hear, or hear mention of the song "Look Down, Look Down That Lonesome Road" it brings back memories of the walk home after church. The words don't apply, but the "feel" of the song fits that dark, dirt country road to a tee. The lamps were unlit because that would have been a waste of coal oil. (There were probably only three or four flashlights in the whole community, and nobody ever had batteries for them.) If there was moonlight or pretty good starlight we could see the ruts and potholes well enough. On a dark night though, or where tree limbs arched over the road, we all walked along in pitch darkness.

Sometimes on the walk to church we would fall in with another family or two, but usually we didn't run into anybody till we got to the church house. People generally arrived at different times, depending mostly on how many cows they had to milk before they left home. After church though, and after everyone had stood around talking for nearly an hour, people going in the same direction left together.

Since everyone was pretty well talked out by then, what conversation there was didn't require any answering back. Sometimes someone would hum or whistle the tune of a hymn that had stuck in his or her head at the service. Or someone would comment that the butterbeans should be ready to start picking in a few days. Since the preacher was no longer within earshot, it was okay to contradict him, so someone might allow as how he had been wrong (or right) about what such-and-such chapter and verse really meant.

Lee and Ophelia lived closest to the church house so we told them good night first as they headed up their lane. Aunt Addie's and Uncle Jack's place was next. If Stella and J.N., or Buster and Ruby, or Aunt Daisy — who all lived beyond our place — hadn't made it to church that night, it was just us for the last half mile. When we got home, everybody went behind their favorite bushes to pee except Grandpa, who made a round to check the cow pen and horse lot. He presumably peed somewhere on his round, but he was so secretive about such functions that I never knew for sure whether he ever had to pee. Then we all went directly to bed.

8
The Church in the Wildwood

Oak Flat and hundreds of other Piney Woods settlements have never had a post office or any kind of store. But all of them had, and still have, at least one church house or a substitute thereof.

When a settlement grew large enough to become a town (and many never did), "proper" churches were built, usually with Sunday school rooms and steeples, and certainly with varnished pews. But country churches can only be described as rustic. Some of the men folks would cut timber in the woods and have it sawed into lumber at a local mill. Because few of these mills had the equipment to plane the lumber, rough-cut planks were used. Likewise, the simple benches with slatted backs and seats that served as pews were built of local lumber. The wood for the pews was taken to a planer mill though in order to protect the backsides of the congregation from splinters. Then, once a pulpit large enough to accommodate a lamp and the preacher's Bible was built, the church was declared finished. It would be many years, if ever, before enough money was raised to paint anything.

In earlier days in Oak Flat and other settlements there were, of course, no church houses or regular services. Mama told of going to "brush arbor" revivals before World War I when she was a girl. They were held when a traveling preacher would come through in the summer after the crops were planted and laid by, but before harvest and cotton pickin' began. Some local men would clear a patch of land down to bare ground and set long pine posts around what would be the perimeter of the arbor. Then they would build a "roof" of brush so everyone could sit in the shade. Word of the revival would get out pretty fast, and people from miles around would load up their wagons with bedding, cooking utensils, and grub to camp out on the brush arbor grounds. The revival lasted for up to a week, and people stayed for as much of it as they could. Some souls were no doubt saved, but the singing and socializing probably drew more folks than any urgent need for salvation.

Later on in Mama's girlhood, a two-room schoolhouse was built in Oak Flat, and church services were held in it. In the late 1930s and 1940s, though, rural schools throughout the U.S. were merged (that is, "consolidated") into large central school facilities being built in towns and larger villages. When the new school buildings in Huntington were completed, busing began for all students living in the surrounding settlements. The two-room schoolhouses were sold or moved, and the one in Oak Flat was moved to the new campus in Huntington and converted into a home economics building. Thus, Oak Flat and settlements like it were once more without a place to hold church services.

When everyone shared a single church house or meetin' place, denominational differences were largely set aside. A Baptist preacher might hold services one Sunday, an Apostolic preacher the next. People might skip church for any number of reasons, but few openly admitted it was because the preacher was of the wrong persuasion. But now, to remedy the lack of a church house in Oak Flats, the Baptists got together and built one of their very own. It differed from the earlier rustic versions only in that they used planed lumber, and painted the building inside and out. The Pentecostals then decided that they needed their own church too. Grandma, one of the staunchest Pentecostals in the settlement, took it upon herself to get one built. And she did. I'll talk more on that later. For now suffice it say that Oak Flat had two painted church houses.

Most people went to the Baptist church, and it eventually grew and prospered enough to add on some Sunday school rooms. Nobody much ever attended the Pentecostal services except dyed-in-the-wool Pentecostals. It was too fundamentalist for most people's taste. Also, lots of folks had cars by then, so some chose to drive into Huntington, or even Lufkin, to church.

The Pentecostals, "Postolics," and Baptists shared a lot of beliefs and requirements. You had to be "borned again" and baptized by immersion (probably in some farmer's stock tank (that is, a stock-water pond) or down at the river. Drinking, dancing, and not observing the Sabbath were cardinal sins. But there the similarities pretty much ended. Females wearing shorts was considered sinful by all, but Pentecostal women were not even supposed to show any part of their legs or wear cosmetics except for talcum powder applied to fleshy parts that could get "gallded" (galled) from sweating and chafing in the summer.

Some fundamentalist churches would occasionally hold a "foot washing" based on Jesus washing the feet of the disciples to show humility. Grandma told of going to a foot washing in a neighboring settlement. Speaking in "tongues" was another important though rare and unpredictable feature of fundamentalist services and, in the Pentecostal Church, a requirement for membership. I was never at a service where anyone spoke in tongues, but my friend Betty Lois was. When I asked her what it sounded like, she tried to imitate it. It sounded like strange words with their syllables run together.

Fundamentalist, "borned again" churches today differ in many ways from those in the olden days. Grandma would have become absolutely apoplectic if she had lived to see the bouffant hairdos and Mary Kay-decorated faces of the wives of today's TV evangelists. Also, the "borned agains" then would not have advertised their state of grace by reminding you of it every chance they got, or by displaying bumper stickers about it, even if bumper stickers had been around then. They would not have approved of tee shirts on women to begin with, even those with silk-screened religious messages that convert one's bosom into a billboard. And, I'll bet they'd rather have listened to an opera than to today's "contemporary Christian" music. They certainly let you know they had "been saved" by their dress and by comments now and then, such as "we're living in the last days" but that was about it. Also, those were the days when liberal versus conservative hot-button political issues did not reach the pulpit level, but we won't get into that.

Just as mainstream denominations more or less ignore such backwoods carrying-ons as foot washings and speaking in tongues, so the country churches didn't bother much with the finer points of citified theology. The grownups' front porch talk sometimes turned to subjects that my childhood mind found too abstract to grasp. One of these was about affidavits ("affadavids"); I didn't understand what they were talking about then, and I still don't know why anybody in the Piney Woods in the olden days needed to discuss them at length. Talk about the Holy Trinity, that is, that the Father, the Son, and the Holy Ghost are a single entity but also three individuals, also left me completely baffled. Uncle Kyle nailed that one down best though when he allowed as how we weren't meant to understand it, so we ought not to even bother trying.

I never heard the term "original sin" (that is, that we are born sinful, thanks to Eve and the apple) till I was grown. As to the related question of whether we are born good or bad, we always took it for granted that we were just plain "borned." Likewise, I doubt if any of us then knew that there was a debate over whether the Jews killed Jesus.

We didn't know much of anything about Jews anyway. We sort of knew they didn't eat pork, but I doubt that anyone had even heard of a Bar Mitzvah or the Torah. The only Jews I knew of in Angelina County, although I'm sure there were a few more, were the family who owned the dry goods store in Lufkin. They ran an honest business and stocked good merchandise, and their store was popular. They were part of the local order of things, and I don't remember that we lumped them in together with Jews in general. It's my recollection though that they stayed pretty much to themselves and nobody really knew them. I don't think it ever entered anybody's head to wonder if they held or attended their own worship services.

As to Jews in general, we held the prevailing notion that they were merchants and most of them lived in big Eastern cities. We also considered it common knowledge that they were stingy and drove a hard bargain (although the same could be said of some of our kinfolks). We were untainted by any other anti-Semitic prejudices.

Catholics were another matter. Almost all backwoods Protestants harbored the whole litany of anti-Catholic — and especially anti-Pope — prejudices. Animosity was directed at the church itself, and not individual Catholics. After all, so conventional wisdom decreed, most of the money that came into the church went straight to "Italy," and Catholics had to pray to Mary instead of Jesus. The anti-Catholic views were the old, familiar ones, but they were still tinged a little from the days when Texas belonged to Mexico. When Stephen and Moses Austin got permission from Mexico for Americans to settle in Texas, one of the conditions was that the colonists convert to Catholicism. Some did convert, or at least went through the motions. For others, freedom of religion was one of the rallying cries in the Texians' revolt against Mexico.

In the days I'm recalling, there were more Catholics than Jews in the area, but not by far. There was a Catholic church in Lufkin, but most people didn't even know a Catholic. In my youngest years, we knew only one. She was the cleaning lady at the Foundry when Daddy worked there. Her name was Maria.

I still remember what Maria looked like. She was short and plump, with twinkling eyes, and always seemed to wear a drab, gray smock of a dress. When I would drop by to see Daddy at his office, which I was allowed to do, she would greet me with smiles and the kind of chitchat one uses with children. I didn't always understand her broken English though. She was also "Mexican," another "category" of people I knew only one of in those days.

Back when Mexico owned Texas (or maybe even when Spain owned Texas), a Catholic mission settlement was established between what is now Lufkin and Nacogdoches. When I was a young'un, it was still a flourishing community. We often drove past it on our way to visit kinfolks in Center. It had a school and a Catholic church and was still very much a typical Mexican village. Its hundred or so residents were descendents of the original settlers from Mexico, and their first language was Spanish.

I was told that Maria was "borned and raised" in this little settlement, as were her parents and several generations of her grandparents. I think she still lived there. If so, I don't know how she commuted to the Foundry, a distance of about ten miles. For all I know, she might have walked. At any rate, she was always at work with her broom and mop when she was supposed to be. Wages of less than twenty dollars a month would have been typical back in those days for that type of work.

Christmas was always a high point in Maria's life, and she shared it with the children of her co-workers in the office. That would have been a handful of young'uns, but she somehow managed to buy each and every one of them a peppermint candy cane. In those days you could get penny canes or nickel canes, and Maria always got the sizable nickel ones. That would have equaled out to a lot of hours pushing the broom. To this day, when I see a peppermint candy cane at Christmas, I think of Maria.

#4 Under the Black Gum
Church Tales

Once upon a time in the Piney Woods, a woman got "borned again" at a revival and, along with all the "Hallelujahs" and such, she started hollerin' out that she could hear Gabriel blowing his horn. All this embarrassed her son, and after church he told her he knew good and well she hadn't heard Gabriel blowing his horn. Her husband then said, "Now, Son, you leave your Ma alone. She might've heard him give it a little toot or two."

Another time, a long-winded preacher was praying for every thing he could think of — all the people in the congregation, their kinfolks, their crops, the weather, the heathens in China, and sinners everywhere. The folks up front in the "saved pews" chimed in with "Yes, Lords" and "Hallelujahs." There was one man in the community, let's call him Brother Smith, who was born with a deformed leg that was too short. When the preacher got around to praying for Brother Smith, he said, "O Lord, let Brother Smith's bad leg grow to be as long as his good leg." Another man in the back of the church who was getting bored blurted out, "Yes, Lord, and longer, too."

Then there was the man who had been going to the revival meetin' every night and had "gotten religion." During this time, one of his cows gave birth to a sickly calf. Grandpa happened to stop by at the man's place late one afternoon and noticed the sick calf. But instead of being out in the cowpen tending to the calf, the man was up at his house getting ready to go to the revival meeting that night. Grandpa, who was well known as the community's substitute for a veterinarian, said to the man, "That calf's goin' to die pretty soon if you don't stay home and tend to it." "Oh, the Lord'll take care of that calf," the man answered as he finished getting ready to go. Grandpa later told us, "Well, the Lord did take care of that calf. He took it up to Heaven to live with Him."

A man by the name of Dick Johnson and his family decided to have a taffy pulling at their house after church one night. Before the service, Mr. Johnson asked the preacher to announce it and tell everyone they were all invited. During the service, the preacher got so carried away trying to save sinners that he forgot all about the announcement until church was over and everyone had started walking out the door. When he remembered, he yelled out, "Wait a minute, y'all! I nearly forgot. Everyone's invited to a big Dick pulling over at Taffy Johnson's tonight!"

9

GRANDMA WADE AND SOME OF HER HUSBANDS

Grandma Wade (Grandma's mama) had four husbands, but unlike James Eason Russell, only one spouse at a time. Mama once said that she thought Grandma Wade had hot pants, but if she did it came and went because she only accumulated a total of 30 married years out of her 90-year lifetime. In other words, she was husbandless for well over half of her adult life.

She was an independent cuss, and maybe she got that way from being on her own so much, or maybe, and this jibes more with the grandmother I remember, she had an independent streak to begin with. At various times during her intermarriage periods she lived as the head of a household on a farm and all alone in an apartment in Nacogdoches. Later she lived in the garage apartment behind her daughter Cora's and son-in-law Merrill's house. Her last residence was in a two room "cabin" in Grandma's and Grandpa's side yard.

When she was in her late 70s, she bought the "cabin" from somebody in Huntington and had it moved out to Oak Flat. She then proceeded to convert it into a "cottage," complete with wallpaper, tar paper exterior siding made to look like bricks, and a yard of its own with flowers (but no bathroom or running water). One room was a kitchen/dining room, but she ate most of her meals with Grandma and Grandpa. Although she wasn't expected to, she earned her keep by doing all the churning and cleaning the privy. She lived there, still hale and hearty, the rest of her life.

A. J. Wade, her third husband, is why our bunch of the family calls her "Grandma Wade." Some family branches refer to her as "Grandma Kate," and the multitude of other friends and relatives she knew during her long life called her "Aunt Kate." (Once in her late 80s she was chatting with a friend at a graveyard working. He said, "Aunt Kate, how old are you now?" When she told him, he said, "Well, there ain't much use in you going home then!")

A YOUNG GRANDMA WADE, CIRCA 1885

Since there aren't any other "Kates" to confuse things in this part of my tale, that's what I'll *mostly* call her here. Also, three husbands are enough to deal with here, so we'll save the fourth one for later.

Kate probably never saw her daddy (John E. Brown), since it seems certain that Granny Hutch was pregnant with her when John E. went off and disappeared during the Civil War. We know of only one possible sibling of Kate's, the "Little Molly" who was mentioned by John E. in his letters and who also disappears from the record. Granny Hutch had married Aaron Hutchinson by the time Kate was five, and they raised her as an only child.

Kate's childhood during the post-Civil War days was typical for backwoods East Texas. Unlike states in the Deep South — Georgia, Louisiana, etc. — Texas was not much affected by the throes of Reconstruction except for widespread depression. Very little cash money circulated, but as they had (and would) for years, folks out in the Piney Woods managed to eke out a living.

So Kate went to school and learned the three R's, which she remembered until her dying day. She learned to milk a cow, tend the garden, work in the field, sew, cook on a wood stove, and all that kind of nostalgic stuff. Somewhere along the line, she picked up and "learned by heart" enough verses and old sayings to fill a farmer's almanac. Some of these were well known and often repeated by all, but some came from who knows where. A major mission in Kate's life was to teach as many of these as possible to every young'un she came into contact with.

Some of these old verses and such probably date back to the Middle Ages in what's now Britain. But some that Kate passed on sound a little too freshly "English" to have made their way with several generations of settlers from Virginia to Tennessee to Texas. I'd bet she learned them from Aaron; he was, if you'll recall, from England.

Some other English imports made their way into Kate's life as well. During Kate's first 38 years, Victoria was queen of Britain. (She reigned for 64 years, from 1837 until she died in 1901.) "Vickie" was primarily a figurehead since Parliament and the Lords of the Realm formulated and carried out policy, but she certainly did influence the periwigged old boys in power. Victorianism spread along with the British Empire until the sun never set upon either. Some Victorian thinking, especially of the sort intended to keep women on the straight and narrow, even reached the hinterlands of the U.S.

A core belief in Victorian times was that women were a bunch of nymphomaniacs who would go into paroxysms of lust at the mere mention of anything even remotely sexually suggestive. This had some strange effects on our language. For instance, in proper conversation, human anatomy was reduced to those parts of the body that could be seen in appropriately dressed ladies and gentlemen. This taboo even extended to "victuals" and is why, until fairly recently, we referred to chicken parts as white meat or dark meat instead of breasts or thighs.

Kate wasn't a straight-laced Victorian, but she did buy into some of it. Once, when I was in my teens, she said to Mama, "Do you think Winifred is virtuous?" This made Mama furious, but she answered politely.

Early on Kate learned tatting, and she tatted off and on for the rest of her life. Back in those days, women did a lot of crocheting and embroidering, but tatting was harder to master and, hence, less common. Women undoubtedly enjoyed such "fancy needlework" but it was also encouraged as a virtuous pastime. After all, a woman juggling a lap full of thread while minding her stitches should have been pretty immune to lustful thoughts.

Tatting involves using a small shuttle and bobbin to turn out fancy lacework and doilies. It has just about become a lost art, maybe because doilies have gone out of fashion, or just maybe because women aren't expected to be as virtuous as they used to be. At any rate, let's go from tat to tit.

Judging from the number of times she told about it, Kate's most memorable childhood experience happened when some Indians passed by on their way somewhere and stopped for a spell. Kate said that one of the Indian women had the biggest tits she'd ever seen, and she couldn't help but start giggling about them. The Indian woman then flew off the handle, grabbed a long butcher knife and took off chasing Kate around and around the house, all the while yelling (and I quote verbatim and phonetically from Grandma Wade) "Hoe bye, hoe bye, slickity bum!" Somebody finally got the buxom woman simmered down, and the Indians left.

Kate, Pat, and Young'uns:

Kate's childhood and youth ended at 17 when she married Patrick Henry ("Pat") Sowell. Back then, most girls had gotten married by the time they were 18, and any that remained single by the age 21 were almost certainly doomed to Old Maidhood. Pat, at 24, was at about the age when young men married. They settled into married life around "Smernie" where both had grown up and still had lots of kinfolks. Kate's, of course, included the Hutchinsons, Browns, and Crows. We don't know about Pat's lineage, except that his daddy's name was John.

In 1882 (two years after they got married), Kate's and Pat's son John was born, and another two years later, my grandma, Leah Azeta. In the Old Testament, "Leah" was both the wife and cousin of Jacob, who was, in turn, the brother of Esau and the son of Isaac. We don't know how Kate and Pat hit upon the middle name of "Azeta." It's from some Indian language and means "White Cloud." Grandma's middle name never came up much, but when it did you could tell she was proud of it.

Things went along smoothly for the family during the next several years except for young John's close shave. There are four kinds of poisonous snakes in the U.S.: rattler, water moccasin, copperhead, and coral snake, and all four live in East Texas. The first three are pit vipers, that is, their venom is stored in pouches on the sides of their heads, sort of where anything else's ears would be. (In fact, the venom "pits" have scrunched out their ears so much that, except for sensing vibrations, the vipers are nearly deaf.)

The coral snake, on the other hand, is neither a pit viper nor does it have fangs. Its teeth curve inward into its mouth, so instead of striking, it has to chomp down on its prey then hang onto it while it spews out a toxin that can kill almost anything in a few minutes. With its bands of red, yellow, and black, it is, I guess, a pretty snake.

One day when John was two or three and playing out in the yard, Kate, from the kitchen, heard him saying, "pretty kitten, pretty kitten." It dawned on her right off the bat that they didn't have any kittens, so she rushed out the back door to see what was going on. Young John was sitting on the ground with a coral snake across his lap, while stroking its back and saying "pretty kitten." Kate was somehow able to knock the snake off John's lap and grab him up in her arms. I don't know what happened to the snake.

The summer of 1889, Kate was pregnant and Pat, at 32, came down with either measles or malaria or the flu and died. Kate had Cora, her third, and last, surviving child, six months later.

Cousin Margaret, Cora's daughter, told me that some folks back then said, and firmly believed, that Cora would have psychic powers because she was born after her daddy died. To put this notion to rest, Margaret said in an uncharacteristic dictatorial voice, "But of course she didn't!"

For eight years after Pat died, Kate lived around "Smernie" with her children. Then she got herself into something that was later to become a deep, dark family secret.

Husband Number Two:

County records show that, in 1897, Kate married a J. C. Simmons. We all knew about her other husbands, but unlike James Eason Russell and his two simultaneous families, which was common knowledge, if anybody knew about Simmons they never even whispered it.

It figures that Kate would have married again. Simmons might have swept her off her feet. (Maybe Mama knew more than she let on when she made her "hot pants" remark.) There would in any case have been practical concerns. Kate was a 34-year-old widow with two teenaged children (John and Grandma) and a seven year old (Cora). It would have been a hardscrabble life.

The next thing we know about her marriage to Simmons is that, three years later, the census shows "Kate Simmons" as head of a household raising her children, but no mention of J.C.

Quite a few years ago, Grandma wrote me a letter briefly describing her family history. She devoted one sentence to Simmons, and I quote, "My mother married a Mr. Simmons who wasn't good to her and she left him." And that's the end of the Simmons affair. It was probably hushed up because virtuous Victorian women just did *not* leave their husbands, no matter how mistreated or two-timed they had been.

So Simmons disappeared as completely as John E. Brown and "Little Molly." Whether they divorced or not doesn't really matter because Kate didn't marry again for over 10 years. If Simmons had headed off for points west or somewhere and hadn't been heard from during that period, he would have been considered dead. Then, if Kate took a notion to, she would have been free to remarry, both legally and virtuously.

Kate Becomes Grandma Wade:

Whenever the differences in spouses' ages came up, which was surprisingly often, Kate would always say, "It's better to be an old man's darling than a young man's fool." Whether she had that experience with a young man in the Simmons affair, I can't say. She must have had experience with an older man, though, because when she married Andrew Jackson Wade, her third husband, in 1910, he was a widower of 64 and she a mere 47.

I always heard "A. J." referred to as Mr. Wade, but I'll skip the niceties here and just call him "Wade." He was from "Smernie," where there were as many Wades as there were Sowells and Browns, and Kate must have known him all her life. If she had visions of living happily ever after with him, it didn't work out that way for very long. They had been married only seven years when Wade died. By then all three of Kate's children were grown, married, and had young'uns of their own.

Kate didn't remarry until about 20 years later. She and Granny Hutch, now also widowed, lived together for several years, probably until Granny

Hutch died. Kate, then in her early 60s, refused all offers from various kinfolks to come stay with them. She rented an apartment all to herself, which suited her just fine, thank you very much.

At one point (at least) in Kate's marriage to Wade, two of his "children" by his first wife were living with them: Flora, who was in her 30's, and Andrew Jr., who was in his late teens. Speaking of age differences, Kate was old enough to have been Andrew Jr,'s mother (but of course she wasn't, as Cousin Margaret would say), but young enough only to have been Flora's sister. Actually it's a little more complicated than that.

An old hillbilly song called "I'm My Own Grandpa" used to be popular, and if you followed through the relationships closely, you would see that the singer was indeed his own grandpa. The situation with Kate and Wade is not that complicated, but it could have been if they'd had children of their own.

Wade's first wife, and the mother of his children was Mary Mollie Crow, the daughter of Jim Crow and Susan Brown, that is, "OldSusanBrownCrow," if you'll recall. Susan was Kate's daddy's sister, and therefore Kate's auntie, which makes Kate and Mary Mollie Wade (Wade's first wife) first cousins. Therefore, Flora, Andrew Jr., and the rest of Wade's young'uns would have been both Kate's stepchildren and second cousins!

GRANDMA WADE (R) AND HER DAUGHTER CORA (L) IN FRONT OF THE CABIN WHERE CORA WAS BORN

#5 Under the Black Gum
Some of Grandma Wade's Verses and Sayings

This one's for choosing up sides for a game of Red Rover, or for someone to be "It" in a game of hide-and-seek:

> "Incie, pincie, cootsie corn,
> Apple core and apple thorn,
> I-want-*you*!"

This one's about climbing trees:

> "Up a hickory, down a pine;
> Split my britches right behind.
> Asked my Mama nice and kind,
> To patch my britches right behind."

There's not much to this one, and you just said it whenever it seemed appropriate:

> "Bread and butter, come to supper."

East Texas Hoot Owls throw in a little soft patter between their "Whooos," so sometimes when we said this one just right, an owl would answer. (I have no idea who Billy and Archie were.):

> "Whoooo! Whoooo! Whoooo cooks for you all:
> Billy and Archie and the Devil and I don't know
> Whooo-all, Whooo-all, Whooo-all."

This just-for-fun one was a favorite of Grandma Wade's:

> "Out West-ess wasp-ess build their nest-ess
> On post-ess as big as your fist-ess."

I've been sitting here pounding on this keyboard till I'm plumb wore out, so I'll wind this up with another old saying that Grandma Wade, and others, used often:

"I'm so T-I-R-D tired, (pronounced tarred)
I could F-A-R-T faint!"

10
LEAH AZETA SOWELL RUSSELL (1884–1976):
HER GROWING UP YEARS

I can sum up Grandma's life in two words: hard work. Of course, lots and lots of folks in the Piney Woods worked hard, but Grandma outworked a bunch of them in terms of the number of working hours she racked up. I guess that'll be partly "the Renfro there were in her." Her main pleasures in life were ice cream, fishing, and going to church. The hunks of time between these were spent working. She started working early and kept at it one way or another throughout her 92 years.

Well into middle age she worked in the field to thin corn, which meant swinging a hoe to slice out the corn stalks that had come up too thick, and to pick cotton, a job that required bending over to pluck out the cotton bolls and stuff them into a long sack. The sack was dragged along the ground by shoulder straps, and got heavier and heavier as more and more cotton got stuffed into it.

After Grandpa died when Grandma was 70, she started making and selling quilts, sunbonnets, and some kind of wastebaskets she made from egg cartons (she sent me the directions for these but I could never figure them out.) When she was in her 80's she started "tending to old people." She once said something about "that old man I'm tending to," and we asked her how old he was. She answered, "Oh, he's about 65."

Since her daddy (Pat Sowell) died when she was five years old, she grew up fatherless except for the brief period when Kate was married to Simmons, for whatever that was worth. Grandma was born and raised in "Smernie," as was Kate, so the little family was surrounded by an abundance of aunts, uncles, and cousins. All these kinfolks helped make up for the lack of a man around the house.

Grandma's early years were not that different from Kate's. She went to school, learned to garden, and so on. Unlike Kate, she never mastered tatting, but she could sew reasonably well. I'd bet that, by the time she was at least ten, she had learned to milk a cow and work in the field.

Grandma was too focused on work and the sweet-by-and-by to give much of a hoot about hanging onto "things" that could be passed on to future generations. We've "saved" some sunbonnets and quilts and some boxes of photographs. Except for that we have only the amber shoe. And we have that only because Mama hung onto it. Made of amber glass, it's etched on the outside in what's known in the antique collector's world as the button and daisy pattern.

When Grandma was a little girl, she was given the shoe by a man who lived down the road from them. He was going to town on horseback one day and stopped to chat. He promised Grandma he would bring her something from town, and sure enough, on his way back he gave her the amber shoe filled with little candies. It didn't hold much candy because it's about the size of an infant's foot, but it would have fitted nicely into his pocket for his ride home.

When Mama and Daddy first set up housekeeping, Grandma gave them the amber shoe. Mama then started a tradition that lasted a little while in the family. When I was born, she put it on my foot. She tried to do the same when my brother Fred was born, but his feet were too big for it. She did put it on the feet of a few nieces and nephews, but by the time my brother Linwood came along, the tradition had died out. That's probably just as well because, unlike Cinderella, I imagine we babies didn't appreciate trying on a glass shoe!

I do have a batch of letters from Grandma. After I was grown and living here and there around the country, we corresponded regularly. She wrote legibly, spelled phonetically, and used fairly good grammar. She didn't believe in punctuation though, and in keeping with the writing style of the olden days, she capitalized *every* Noun. Mostly she wrote about the daily comings and goings, but occasionally she would throw in something more substantial. In one of these cases she was telling about "Smernie" (which she spelled correctly), and wrote:

> "Old Smyrna is where me and my brother went to school. Part of the time we walked and sometimes we went horseback. He had a pretty little horse and we both rode him."

She would have ridden sidesaddle since that's what females were supposed to do; they couldn't have ridden astride anyway unless they were brazen enough to hike their long skirts up to their navels. I picture that Grandma would have gotten on first so she could sit sideways and crook one leg around the saddle horn. Her brother John could then have clambered up behind. He could have reached around her to handle the reins, still a common way of riding double. Or Grandma could have handled the reins herself. A lot of women back then didn't know anymore about riding a horse than most of today's women do. Grandma could, and did, ride though, and a story she told when she was about 70 bears this out.

When she was in her latter teens, but not yet married, a social of some sort was to be held in a settlement a fair piece away. Heavy rains in the days before the social had caused flooding, and a big creek on the way to that settlement had overflowed its banks. Grandma never did much that was frivolous, but she made up her mind to go to the social, come hell or high water. She said she went by horseback, alone I think, and forded the creek on the horse. Unless the floodwaters went down pretty fast, she would have done the same in reverse on the way back. I've never known when or how she first met Grandpa. But I'd like to think he went to that social too.

LEAH AZETA SOWELL RUSSELL, CIRCA 1910

11
WILLIAM ELI RUSSELL (1875–1952): HIS GROWING UP YEARS

If I'd had to pick one person to be stranded with on a desert island, it would have been Grandpa. He could have rigged up a shelter in short order and, by sunset, a fire would have been smoldering with enough hot coals to cook the fish he'd snared. But best of all, his quips about our predicament would have kept us chuckling.

Like most young folks out in the country in those days, Grandpa went through about the eighth grade. Classes didn't go beyond that in the one-room schools, but students who did their lessons learned the three R's, some civics, history, and geography, and to the extent of the teacher's knowledge, some science. (When Mama was in school, vitamins had just been "discovered," and she said somebody asked the teacher what they were; she said he stammered and then answered, "Why, that's like salt and pepper!")

Grandpa picked up pieces of scientific knowledge here and there all his life. He once described to me the life cycle of horse flies. They start out as nits, that is, the yellow, pin-head sized eggs that stick to horse's hair. Then they hatch into bots, a sort of tiny, yucky worm that burrows beneath the horse's skin. In their final stage they break out as horse flies and bite, breed, lay more nits, and die.

Grandpa learned a lot of things they didn't teach in school. He learned to plow, shoot, ride a horse, and tend to and doctor all kinds of livestock. He learned to keep bees and tend to the hives, and to get to the wild plum trees or the wild magnolias or persimmons in the woods, whether a trail led to them or not, without getting lost. Somebody gave him a pocket compass one Christmas, but he never used it except to show folks how it worked.

People all over the area (including me!) looked up to Grandpa as a sort of homespun hero. He never took advantage of his reputation though, nor let it go to his head. Maybe spending his earliest years dressed in a smock taught him the virtue of modesty.

Until relatively recently there was no such thing as special clothes for children. As far back as the Middle Ages in Europe, children, both boys and girls, were dressed in a sort of skirted, slip-on over the head type of tunic until they were at least five. After that they graduated to smaller-sized versions of adult clothes. This custom lasted through the 1700s in most places, and through the 1800s in the Piney Woods.

Grandpa said he was a big young'un before they let him quit wearing smocks. They didn't wear underwear beneath a smock, and Grandpa told me that before he advanced to wearing britches he was old enough to be embarrassed about "showing his butt." He said he stuffed rocks into the hem of the smock to hold it down when the wind blew.

One time, though, Grandpa showed his butt good and proper. When he was in his teens he and two other boys were taking a load of corn to the gristmill to be ground into meal. They had to cross a fair-sized creek and, even though it was early spring and the water still cold, they decided to go skinnydipping. But just as they were supposed to all jump in at the same time, one of the boys chickened out. Grandpa and the third boy took off after him with the idea of pummeling him around a little bit. All three were so intent on their running and chasing that they didn't pay any attention to where they were. Before they knew it they'd ended up buck naked in a neighbor's farm lot with several people gawking at them.

Grandpa started learning to plow not too long after he started wearing britches. Besides being hard work, plowing with a team of mules or horses requires brainwork, alertness, stamina, and strength. It'd be easier if you had a third hand for holding the reins while you used your other two for gripping the plow handles to sink the blades into the earth. Three eyes would help too; one focused on the furrow, one on the team, and the other on where you're headed. Plowing with a team of oxen, which folks did back then, requires you to be even more nimble.

The oxen used for draft animals are castrated (or "cut") males, the same thing as steers except the word "steer" refers to a "male" beef cow. Nobody since antiquity has been able to figure out how to design a bridle that would work on an ox, so there are no reins. You control an ox team by "steering" the boss-man ox, called the near ox, and the other oxen follow his lead. There are several ways of doing this. The near ox can be guided by a single rope attached to a halter or nose ring or simply looped securely around his horns. This works well for a pair of oxen pulling a plow or small wagon. The big timber wagons out in the woods, however, required teams of up to four pairs of oxen.

The near ox was always hitched at the front left (looking forward), and the driver walked along beside him. A well trained near ox responded pretty well to hollered out commands, namely, "whoa come 'ere" to go left and "yea back" to go right. The driver always carried a short whip on a long "handle" (that is, stock) to use when all else failed. An errant ox would be prodded with the end of the stock or smacked across the rump, as gently as possible, with the whip end. The ox to the side of the near ox is called the "off ox."

(I once read a magazine article that used the term "Adam's old fox." A reader's letter later said that that was incorrect — which it is — and that it should be "Adam's old ox," also incorrect. It should be "Adam's off ox," and I don't know from Adam's off ox how that expression got started.)

At any rate, by the time Grandpa was in his late teens he could handle just about any kind of team, and he hired on with a timber company to, among other things, drive a log-wagon. During this period he batched (that is, "bachelored") with another young logger in a cabin way out in the woods.

The other man took off a few days one time to visit his family, and was due back on such and such a day. The day came, it got dark, and he still hadn't shown up. It got later and later, with still no sign of him. Grandpa went to bed and went to sleep, but woke up when he heard the man ride up and start unsaddling the horse in the corral. Grandpa expected him to come into the cabin pretty shortly, but he didn't. After some more time went by and the man hadn't come back in, Grandpa got worried and went out to see if anything was wrong. The horse was in the corral, unsaddled, but the man was nowhere to be seen. Grandpa looked and looked, called, and waited. Still no sign of the man. He never did show up. He just plain vanished from the face of the earth.

Maybe that shook Grandpa up enough that he decided to move back to "civilization." Or maybe, by then, he had earned enough to buy a place of his own. He was always a ladies' man, but the next thing I know about him is that he was courting pretty seriously.

12
RIDING THE RING

Let's go a ways back here for a bit to the really olden days, not just the plain old olden days, but to medieval times. This period lasted roughly a thousand years with its beginning usually pegged at the collapse of the Roman Empire in the West. By the year 300 A.D., the Romans had conquered all of northern Africa, the Middle East, Europe (except what's now Germany because the natives kept beating them back), and England. By 400 A.D., the Empire had ceased to exist in its former guise due partly to the rise of Christianity, partly to a series of scheming politicians, psychotic emperors, and pure-D ninnies, but most of all because the Empire had gotten too big to manage.

In the 330s, the Emperor Constantine, who seems to have been fed up with all of the above, tried to get things back on track. He formally endorsed Christianity and outlawed the persecution of Christians. (It's not clear whether he was a professing Christian, but he did get baptized on his deathbed.) In 331 he moved the capitol of the Empire from Rome to Constantinople (now Istanbul, in Turkey). With the capitol so far away, the Empire lost control of Western Europe and Britain not long after that.

With the loss of central control from Rome, Western Europe and Britain went through a 500-year period of what we would today call nation building and insurgency. Wars, of course, went on even longer but, by 1,000 A.D., there were established governments (even if they did, and do, get toppled from time to time). It's no coincidence that King Arthur is said to have lived at the beginning of the medieval period, that is, in the early 500s. There is debate as to whether he was a real man or the hero of a myth, so he is usually dubbed by historians as semi-legendary. At any rate, his real purpose in life (if indeed he existed) was to unite Britain into a nation. According to the legends, he was killed in battle in 537, but he (or others) did get Britain headed off toward nationhood.

What comes to mind most, though, when we think of King Arthur and medieval times is a bunch of knights and their pages riding around saving damsels in distress, slaying dragons, and seeking the Holy Grail. There were real castles and knights and their ladies, and maybe even a dragon or two during this era, but also ambitious lords, chieftains, and upstarts all scheming and fighting to become king. The knights didn't have to wait long for a good, bloody battle, but there were some quiet intervals in between. During these lulls they traveled around to tournaments.

Such shindigs, held by the lord of some manor or some town eager for tourists, drew big crowds. There was the aroma of horses and the clang of armor as knights showed off their fighting skills in mock combat. Many a maiden was wooed (and maybe even bedded), musicians strummed their lutes, and jesters went around acting silly. The whole shebang wasn't much different from what we'd have today if we combined a football game and a rock concert.

Of all the competitive events held at a tournament, the jousts were probably the most exciting. Two knights with long, blunted lances would ride full tilt at one another, each aiming to knock the other off his horse. Much sparring, jabbing, fending off, clanging, and booing and cheering went on before one of the knights was finally unseated. The winner was given some kind of a prize, which he presented to the fair maiden of his choice.

By the end of the middle ages knighthood was no longer in flower. Knights had phased over from being heroic fighters to serving on governmental councils and were more expert at wielding quill pens than lances. Tournaments and jousting had become history except for a few scattered events held here and there. But they lived on in a gentler form and were held in at least one place almost a thousand years later. And that place was East Texas!

In the late 1800s into the early 1900s, long before high school basketball, senior proms, or even rodeos had made it to the Piney Woods, young men strutted their stuff "Riding the Ring." A big circle would be cleared to bare ground around which stout posts were driven at regular intervals. Metal iron rings, probably "borrowed" from wagon harnesses, were dangled — one to each post. One man at a time rode the ring on horseback with a long wooden pole as a stand-in for a lance. The objective was to ride the ring at a good gallop and "spear off" as many of the iron rings on the wooden pole as possible. The man with the most rings on his lance and the fastest time was declared the winner. He received a token prize, which, according to custom, he gave to the fair maiden of his choice.

For the term paper in one of my English classes in college, I had to research a subject in the library and write a proper report on it. The instructor laid out a whole batch of "you musts": for instance, choose your own topic, find and read at least three books on the subject (not including encyclopedias), provide a bibliography, footnotes, and the works. Mama had told me how riding the ring used to be popular, and how it was a holdover from medieval times, so I chose that as my topic. I did find and read the required three books. (They are now out of print.) Each went into varying detail about how riding the ring did indeed date back to medieval jousts, and how the custom made its last stand in East Texas (just so you'll know I didn't make all this up out of thin air). I wrote what I thought was a sterling term paper, but the teacher gave me a C on it because she didn't like the topic. (She may be posthumously giving me F's on this whole missive for not providing footnotes!)

Now back to the plain old olden days. Recall that as we left Grandpa and Grandma several pages back, he was seriously courting the ladies, and she was hankering enough to go to the social that she forged a raging creek on horseback to get there. Somewhere between those pages Grandma was one of the young ladies Grandpa was courting. At some point in here, a "Riding the Ring" was held and Grandpa entered the competition.

Folks from miles around went, including Grandma and lots of other eligible maidens. Grandpa was always a fine horseman, and he won the competition hands down. He had been paying some serious attention to Grandma, but he must have thought she wasn't responding sufficiently. When the time came to give his prize to the fair young maiden of his choice, he rode right past Grandma and gave it to another lass. (Mama said that the young lady Grandpa gave the prize to was a Carrell; I don't remember her first name.) This made Grandma so jealous and mad that she decided she'd better "corral" him right quick.

On the ninth of March 1901, they got married. They lived happily some of the time ever after.

Top - Eli and Leah Sowell about the time they married
Bottom - An older Eli and Leah Russel, circa late 1920s

13

Eli and Leah's Young Family

Two years after Grandpa and Grandma married, a bouncing baby girl arrived that they named Lillian (no middle name) and I call Mama. Her early years weren't much different from Abe Lincoln's except that she did her homework with pencil and paper instead of on a slate, and near a coal-oil lamp instead of by light from the fireplace. From these backwoods beginnings though, Mama's life, and to a lesser extent her siblings' lives, spanned one of the most noteworthy periods in history.

Mama was born in 1903, the year the Wright Brothers flew the first powered aircraft at Kitty Hawk. Also that year, Pierre and Marie Curie won the Nobel Prize for their research into radioactivity. Some daring souls made the first crossing of the U.S. by car (it took 65 days), and Henry Ford founded the Ford Motor Company. Marconi had transmitted radio messages in Morse code from Newfoundland in Canada to Cornwall in England. Freud was at work developing the field of psychoanalysis, and Einstein on his theories of relativity. Changes of other sorts were also peeking up over the horizon. For instance, a woman in New York was arrested for smoking a cigarette in public.

In 1906, the year of the San Francisco earthquake, Mama's sister Winnie came along. The next year Oklahoma became the 46th state. When the girls were seven and four, respectively, Halley's comet made a spectacular visit. Mama told of remembering it being as bright, but bigger, than a full moon. Two years later, Arizona and New Mexico became states, and a Polish chemist named Kasimir Funk coined the term "vitamine" (his spelling). And Mama, at nine, was getting old enough to help out in the field, while Aunt Winnie wouldn't have to swing a hoe for a couple more years. In one of Grandma's rare spurts of reminiscing she wrote to me in the early 1970s that, and I quote verbatim, along with her lack of punctuation:

> "she (Lillian) was so much help to us she wasn't a bit lazy (and) use to take her little hoe and go with me to the field &

work as hard as I did(.) Winnie was sweet and good but kinder lazy(.)"

In many ways, except maybe in terms of laziness, the two girls were identical. They looked so much alike that it's hard to tell which one is which in some of the old photos. They were both tall and skinny; in fact, Grandpa once told Mama her legs were so skinny they were apt to break off and stick in her. Both had friends galore, and both played the piano, although Aunt Winnie was by far the best musician. (In her later days, Mama would occasionally sit down at the piano when she was feeling blue and peck out a soulful rendition of "Carry Me Back to Old Virginie".)

Although the girls began doing their share of the work early on, they still played such standard old-timey games as hopscotch. They didn't have any store-bought toys but they did have "play pretties," that is, anything they could latch onto and pretend it was something else. They rolled and tied together cornhusks to serve as dolls, and cut pictures out of old Sears, Roebuck catalogs to use as paper dolls. Mama said that one of her prized possessions was a fancy little box with a bright-colored picture on it. One time a family with a retarded son, I think his name was Debs, came to see them. Debs got ahold of the box and, when it was time for the family to leave, he wouldn't return it. When his family told him he had to give it back to Lillian, he said, "I never do get nothin' and Aye God I'm goin' to have this." (Mama did eventually get the box back.)

The girls also pulled pranks. One time, when the family was going to town, Aunt Winnie had to pee but Grandpa told her she'd have to hang on till he came to a good place to stop the wagon. When she couldn't hang on much longer, Mama told her to just jump off the wagon and crawl under it and squat. Then when she finished she could crawl out and jump back on the wagon. Mama knew that even though a wagon feels like it's barely moving, in fact the team's pulling it at a slightly faster clip than an adult can walk. In her haste Aunt Winnie didn't consider this, though, so off the wagon she jumped. But just as she had squatted and let loose, the wagon rolled right on past her and left her squatting butt up for all to see in the middle of the road.

1914 marked the arrival of another addition to the family, sister Mary Katherine. Aunt Mary would thereafter remain Mama's "little sister," and indeed she kept her sense of playfulness throughout her life. In the world outside the Piney Woods, the Federal Income Tax was enacted, the Panama Canal opened, the brassiere was patented, and World War I broke out in Europe. (The U.S. didn't enter it until 1917 after German saboteurs blew up a munitions arsenal in New Jersey.) But back "at home," with a new baby in the family Mama, at age 11, had to pitch in more, including helping with milking.

Mama hated milking, especially in winter. She told me how painful it was to squeeze a cow's tits with hands pink and raw from the cold (I never heard of anyone wearing gloves when milking) and how milking agitated even the most docile cows because their tits were cold too. Sometimes, she said, the cow would kick and shuffle around and step on her feet.

In 1915, when Mama was 12, a phone call from Alexander Graham Bell to Dr. Thomas Watson made headlines all over the world. Local telephone service became available in many cities by about 1900, and coast-to-coast messages could be transmitted in Morse code over the telegraph network. Bell's phone call made news because, from New York, he was actually talking to Watson in San Francisco. Even folks in the Piney Woods heard about it. But for years and years, a long distance phone call got folks' adrenaline churning since it meant a far-flung relative had either died or was about to.

A couple of years later, the headlines spread the news that the U.S. had entered World War I. Less prominent parts of the papers also carried blurbs about a new fad. Women in some big cities were bobbing their hair! Some people everywhere claimed that only a brazen hussy would shear her locks, and the righteous, especially in the backwoods, went even further. They allowed as how all the shameless women and the "shooting across the waters" meant the Old Devil himself was at work and that the end was at hand. It took a while but, in spite of this, bobbed hair did catch on in the Piney Woods, including with Mama and Aunt Winnie.

On the 11th hour of the 11th day of the 11th month in 1918, the armistice ending World War I was signed. That same year women over 30 in Britain got the right to vote, and Aunt Mary had her fourth birthday. On the darker side, the soon to be dreaded and feared "Spanish" flu broke out.

Even in those times, before air travel provided germs with a quick way to spread, in its first two years that strain of flu killed 20 million people worldwide. (Back then, that would have been about equal to killing everybody in Texas and in good-sized parts of neighboring states.) By the time the pandemic ended in 1920, it had wiped out more than 50 million people around the globe. And even the Piney Woods had not been spared. I don't know of any of our kinfolks who died of the flu, but in every settlement there were scores who did.

Mama told me that, in many Oak Flat households, no one could care for sick family members because they were all flat on their backs with the flu. She said anyone who had gotten over the flu, and was thus immune, went and stayed with neighbors to tend to their sick. Mama was 15 when the flu broke out, and she said she got over it pretty quick, then spent many a day and night nursing sick neighbors. She told how some died, usually in the night, and then she had to "dress out the corpse," that is, wash and dress it and get it ready for burial. (I often think about how drastic a rite of passage that would have been for a teenaged girl.)

Dr. Rogers (Uncle Merrill, Aunt Cora's husband and Grandma's brother-in-law) had his hands full during the flu pandemic but, as the story goes, he didn't lose a single patient. That might be a dab exaggerated, but it's probably true that he lost very few. I've heard two versions of this. Cousin Margaret, his daughter, said he came up with the ingredients for a flu medicine, which his brother, Uncle "Lunkie" the pharmacist, then compounded for Uncle Merrill's patients. Unfortunately, nobody remembers what was in it.

The other version claims that Uncle Merrill let the fever from the flu run its course "un-doctored," and the heat from the fever killed the flu virus. That may sound like the "kill'em or cure'em" approach, but modern medical thinking is now getting around to recognizing that the reason we have fever is to burn out microbes.

Grandma's and Grandpa's last child, a bouncing baby boy they named Dale, arrived the same year (1919) that the Constitution was amended to make Prohibition the law of the land. Our Founding Fathers set out provisions in the Constitution for amending it, but at the same time they tried to make sure it couldn't be amended based on some willy-nilly whim. First, a proposed amendment must be passed by a two-thirds vote of both houses of Congress or by two-thirds of either all state legislatures or state constitutional conventions. Then, to become law, three-fourths of the states must ratify the proposed amendment. So amending the Constitution requires a groundswell of tsunami proportions.

Prior to Prohibition, drinking had gotten out of hand, and even the Piney Woods had its share of drunken fights and, sometimes, killings. The people sermonizing against Demon Run saw a lot of that kind of thing, but Prohibition certainly did not lead to a nation of teetotalers, thanks to the bootleggers and mobsters. So, 14 years later (in 1933), the country went through the whole business of proposing and ratifying another Constitutional amendment ending Prohibition.

Uncle Dale and Aunt Mary, the two youngsters in the Russell family, grew up a lot like their older sisters had except for one modern convenience. When they were fairly big young'uns, Grandpa bought a car and both he and Grandma learned to drive. Back then cars didn't go very far without some kind of problem, so when folks went anywhere they expected the worst.

When Uncle Dale and Aunt Mary were riding to town with Grandma, they would reach out the window and beat on the outside of the car so it sounded like the whomping of a flat tire. Grandma would then slam on the brakes in the middle of the road and get out to see which tire had gone flat. Since Grandma's faith didn't extend to the behavior of automobiles, they pulled this prank several times before she caught on.

When motor vehicles became more commonplace, another modern convenience of a sort made it to the backwoods. To eke out a living, some poor soul (usually a man) would stock a car or truck with a few basic necessities (flour, coffee, tobacco, needles, thread, a few candy canes and cookies) and make weekly rounds of the settlements. We must have considered this "peddler" some kind of an outcast; I don't think anybody knew him by name, or where he lived, or even if he had a wife and family. I do know that everybody eagerly awaited his visit whether they bought anything from him or not.

One day when Uncle Dale was about ten, he was sitting behind the wheel of the family's parked car and, as young'uns have been known to do, messing around with the pedals and buttons. Just at that point the peddler drove up and Uncle Dale got so excited he threw the clutch into neutral. The car, of course, began to roll. As Grandma was high-tailing it over to check out the peddler's wares, it rolled right into her and knocked her down. Uncle Dale ran over and kept asking, "Mama, Mama, are you hurt?" as he helped her get up. When everybody decided she was okay, Uncle Dale said to her, "Let me buy you some gingersnaps from the peddler."

When Uncle Dale reached dating age (I'm jumping way ahead here), he ran into a problem that gingersnaps wouldn't fix. He became enamored of a pretty girl in the area and began to court her. He said Grandpa took him aside right quick and told him something that nipped the whole affair in the bud: the young lady was a close cousin from James Eason Russell's illegitimate side of the family. Uncle Dale said that other family members also ran into this same situation and that one of Aunt Addie's sons was so heartbroken he almost couldn't break off the relationship.

Long before Uncle Dale and Aunt Mary reached courtin' age though, back in the era of bobbed hair and Prohibition, Mama had reached courtin' age. She was in high school, but she wasn't interested in having a serious beau. She played on the girl's basketball team; she had bobbed hair and wore a very modest "female" sports uniform complete with long bloomers. She was certainly popular, since she always made friends wherever she went. She always loved to dance, but I doubt that school dances existed then.

LILLIAN RUSSELL (FAR RIGHT) AND HUNTINGTON GIRL'S BASKETBALL TEAM, CIRCA 1920S

    A popular song at that time titled "How You Gonna Keep'em Down on the Farm After They've Seen Paree" referred to "doughboys" who had served in France during the war. Mama had not seen "Paree," of course, or even Houston, but she'd made up her mind she wasn't going to spend the rest of her life slaving on a backwoods farm. As I've said, she hated milking. She never mentioned disliking fieldwork, but I'm sure she did. I know she also wanted "finer" things than a fancy box with a picture on it, and she didn't want to worry about such things as when she'd get a new pair of shoes.

    Until Mama was up into her teens she, as well as all other young'uns, went barefooted beginning in early spring. They went barefooted to school, to town, and sometimes even to church. This cut down on the shoe bill, but when the weather got frosty in November, it was okay to start accumulating some shoe mileage. Besides, grownups insisted that young'uns wear shoes then lest they catch cold, or worse, pneumonia. But some young'uns did sneak around and go barefooted in winter. Mama said that to keep from wearing out her shoes, on winter mornings she would put them on but, as soon as she got out of sight of the house, she would take them off and hide them behind a log, then head off to school.

Under the Black Gum Tree

In 1920, at 17, Mama was an adult (recall that 16 was the marrying age for many girls); she had worn shoes year round for a few years (except maybe around the house) and was in the distinct minority of high school graduates. In that same year, a Constitutional Amendment again became the law of the land. Although women agitated and demonstrated for it, not a single one of them voted for it at any of its legal hurdles. It was passed by an all-male vote because, prior to its passage, women in the U.S. could not vote except in local elections in a few western states. This 19th amendment gave women equal voting rights with those of men. Mama could look forward to casting her first ballot when she turned 21 (that would have been 1924 when Coolidge defeated J.W. Davis for the presidency) but, more immediately, she was looking forward to going off to college.

Back then young folks kept what they called a "memory book," that is, an autograph book in which folks wrote them a note, often in verse form. I have Mama's memory book from the early 1920s in which dozens of people wrote entries running the gamut from the corny to the sentimental. I find one that has no punctuation especially touching, and I quote:

> "My own dear Lillian,
> When you turn to this page think of dear Mother and know that she is thinking of you and wishing you much success in your school work and praying for the time to pass off that you can be back home and fill the vacancy in our home(.) many lonely hours there will be for me but hope that you will be happy and contented and remember Mother always and be good (.)
> Mother(.)"

#6 UNDER THE BLACK GUM
IN THE FUST AND FO'MST PLACE

When folks stopped by the house early of a morning to borrow some sugar or the post-hole digger or to just stop for a few minutes on the way to town, we greeted one another with "Y'all all right this mornin'?"

The frequent answer, "We're tolerable," translates into "Not very good, but I'll spare you the details." One morning, though, a neighbor we called Mr. Lowe did not spare any details.

That morning had started out bad when his wife, Hester, threw an old gourd vine into a trash fire she had going. One of the gourds exploded and spewed hot embers into her face, burning it pretty badly. And things didn't get a whole lot better after that.

Mr. Lowe had been raised in the Carolinas and Georgia and had never lost his Deep South accent, so when asked, "Y'all right this mornin'?" he answered, "Well, in the fust and fo'mst place, Hesta busted a goad in her face."

So, in the "fust and fo'mst place," before we pack Lillian off to college, let's look at the Piney Woods way of life she's fixing to leave, but which she returned to one way or another the rest of her life, sometimes if only through the melody of her soulful renditions of "Carry Me Back to Old Virginie."

14

Vittles and Grub

Being as how I'm telling Texas tales, I ought to say folks ate beef and beans from chuck wagons. But in the Piney Woods they certainly did not. And though it may seem odd now, in the olden days what they ate advertised their social (and economic) status far more than what they wore. For example, in about the 1940s, a prominent dentist in Lufkin who enjoyed gardening made it clear to everyone that he grew high-falutin' vegetables and not the sort grown by country hicks.

Back then, as well as now, folks craved some fresh greens to go along with their winter grub. Collards filled this bill to a tee. They grow well almost all winter in the lower South, and although "proper" folks eat collards now, they long ranked as poor folks' fare or even lower. Collards belong to the cabbage family, as does kale, which resembles collards, especially in its young leafy stage. Until fairly recently, though, folks in the Piney Woods thought of kale as some kind of exotic Yankee dish, if they'd ever heard of it at all.

This dentist lived on a busy street, and his garden filled his side yard and so was visible to all passersby. He must have gotten comments about what he was growing because one day a huge sign appeared at the garden's front fence stating:

THIS IS KALE — NOT COLLARDS!

Over the years, Piney Woodsians have eaten a mountain-sized quantity of black-eyed peas plus heaps of other kinds of vittles, including cornbread. In fact, back in the olden days, when folks spoke of their daily bread, they meant cornbread. (A Piney Woods old timer recently described a woman who was "mentally challenged" as "her corn bread don't get brown on top.") Cornbread became the "daily bread" because wheat won't grow worth a hoot in the South, thus flour cost more than meal because it had to be store-bought. Corn grows fine though, so in the early settlements folks either ground their own or took it to the local gristmill. Long after the gristmills had been abandoned, cornmeal was still cheaper than flour. Besides, before they headed westward, our really early ancestors back in Virginia and the Carolinas packed the necessity of cornbread smack into our cultural baggage. Until around the mid-1940s, the word "bread" meant cornbread. The standard white wheat-flour loaf we are used to now was called "light bread," and was considered an extravagance.

Folks did splurge for flour, though, for their breakfast biscuits. Only families so dirt poor, even by Piney Woods standards, that they couldn't afford flour for biscuits ate cornbread for breakfast. They usually hushed this up, however, because they would have been politely branded as "pitiful," or, if they were shiftless and no account, as "sorry."

Rather than saying a family was pitiful or sorry, a more indirect, but insulting, way of getting the point across was to say they ate "rabbit and clabber." I never heard tell of anybody, not even the poorest of the poor, who actually ate rabbit and clabber, but some folks did like clabber. (It's what Little Miss Muffett ate as she sat on her tuffet.) The word is Gaelic and dates back to the Middle Ages in Scotland and Ireland. It means curdled milk, so it's on its way to cottage cheese, yoghurt, or butter. Another word from way back in the Middle Ages used commonly in East Texas, even now to some extent, is "blinky," which describes milk that will soon become clabber.

In the Piney Woods, folks churned after fresh milk had clabbered and the curds and whey had just begun to separate. Churning before this point yields only a few tookie little old blobs of butter; churning very much later results in a rancid mess. The time it takes for the milk to reach this point, or, as the saying went, "for the churning to turn," depends on the temperature.

Folks poured the strained fresh milk right into the churn and then set it aside. In summer the churning usually turned by the next day no matter where it was; in winter it could take a couple of days or so even if it had been set down behind the cook stove. When it had turned, the "churner" (almost always an able female) proceeded to beat on the "milk" with the dasher until the butterfat molecules gave up and clumped together.

The dasher consisted of a broom handle-sized stick that poked up through a hole in the churn's lid. Two sturdy wooden slats shaped like a plus sign formed the business end at the bottom of the dasher. It could take a half hour or more of plunging the dasher up and down for the butter to form. This was easy for the first 10 minutes or so while the "milk" was still thin. After the butter began to thicken up, though, it took a pretty strong arm to keep going. An experienced churner could just about tell by feel when every possible smidgen of butter had "come," as folks used to say.

A three-gallon churn, the size most folks had, yielded somewhat over a pound of butter at about the consistency of half-melted ice cream. What had not turned into butter would have turned into buttermilk, on which the soupy butter floated. This butter was then scooped out onto a clean cloth and the liquid residue squeezed out of it. These squeezings were usually fed to the cats. The "squoze" butter was then transferred to a bowl, patted down, and smoothed out with the back of a spoon. The churning chore was now finished except that the buttermilk had to be poured into its own crock, and the churn and dasher had to be washed and scalded in boiling water.

(Once Aunt Addie was churning when a "city girl" cousin of ours, just relocated to the Piney Woods, stopped by to visit her. Having spent most of her young life at East Coast schools, our cousin had been deprived of countrified knowledge. One of her first questions to Aunt Addie was, "Why are you beating on that bowl with a broom handle?")

Except for a dab of coffee cream and such, most of a family's milk supply went into the churn, so buttermilk was the standard for drinking. If you wanted the "other kind," you had to ask for "sweet milk." And to be polite you would ask for "sweet milk, please, if you've got any." Buttermilk was also the standard for making cornbread and biscuits. (To my way of thinking, if these aren't made with buttermilk, you might as well eat Twinkies.) If you want to cook with buttermilk, you can follow your sweet-milk recipe and add some baking soda. And, if you're fixing cornbread, make sure it gets brown on top!

Along with eggs, and bacon and sausage (until the supply in the smokehouse ran out), you had to have syrup ("surp") to sop your breakfast biscuits in. It took at least two pans of biscuits because everyone ate at least three or four, and I've seen menfolks and stout women eat five, six, or even seven. For some reason, most folks had to make their biscuits and syrup "come out even." That is, if you had some of either left when you'd eaten up the other, you took another helping of the one you'd eaten up. This could lead to a chain reaction of pigging out on both.

Cane syrup was the favorite but, if there wasn't any, molasses was okay. Both are made from sugar cane, which is first pressed and its sweet watery juice collected. Both types of "syrup to be" are then boiled to steam off the water. Except for "bottling," this ends the process for cane syrup, but the syrup maker has to know exactly when it has boiled just long enough to thicken, but not simmered so long that it begins to form sugar crystals. The resulting syrup is clear and a just tad thicker than maple syrup. Molasses is boiled until it does form sugar, then the syrup and the sugar are separated. At this point, the molasses is thick and brownish and is usually poured up into casks where it thickens and darkens some more. (And of course, as everyone knows, it becomes thicker in January.)

Since making cane syrup is a straightforward process, in the olden days some folks made their own, but more often a syrup maker in the area made and sold good-sized batches of it. The cane can be pressed in a homemade hand-operated contraption, and the juice can be boiled down in any good-sized iron vessel; the iron wash pot was often used. The syrup was "bottled" in paint-can-like buckets ranging in size from a pint to a gallon. Molasses, on the other hand, involves too complex a process for a backwoods operation, so has long been a by-product of large-scale sugar-making businesses.

While cane syrup was the staple, we also had honey or jelly on our biscuits from time to time. Grandpa always kept a few beehives that produced a pretty tasty honey, plus, we young'uns loved to chew on the combs until nothing was left but dry wax. Grandpa sometimes raided a wild hive out in the woods. Once he brought in a good-sized syrup bucket filled with comb and an overly dark-colored honey from a wild hive. We tried it, but the comb was as papery as a wasp's nest, and the honey had a bitter, sort of medicinal taste. Those bees must've had a bad year.

Very few of us now know, or remember, that what something eats can affect how its "product" tastes. For instance, a weed called, appropriately enough, bitterweed, grows rampant in East Texas. It's a member of the chamomile family and has yellow pea-sized, petal-less blooms. Sometimes the cows would eat a "bate," that is, a batch, of it, and their milk and butter would be so bitter that even the cats and dogs turned up their noses.

Jellies, made from whatever kinds of fruits or berries we could get a hold of, were always popular. In summer we picked blackberries, dewberries (a larger, sweeter, type of blackberry), huckleberries (something like a small blueberry), and muscadines in the woods. We seldom found many huckleberry bushes, though, so they were a rare treat. Muscadines, a type of wild grape, grow on vines that can climb to the top of a tall tree. We ate them off the vine, but they're so astringent that they'd pucker up the inside of our mouths if we ate too many. With enough sugar though, they make a fine tart jelly that's becoming popular again.

May haws also make a fine jelly, but collecting them is not easy.

They're from May haw trees which grow in wet, soggy river and creek bottoms. In the olden days the fruit, that is, May haw berries, was collected only in wet years when the bottomlands had become swamps. Then the ripe berries would fall off the trees and float on the water below. In a "good May haw year," a few folks would row out into the swamp in a skiff and scoop up the berries and sell them.

Along with all the biscuits, syrup, eggs, and such, there was, of course, coffee. Folks usually didn't fool around with dripolators or percolators, but boiled their coffee instead. (No, I don't remember anyone dropping eggshells in it to settle the grounds, nor do I remember there being any grounds in what we drank.) It was, as the saying went, stronger than studhorse piss with the foam farted off, and also hot enough to boil an egg. Folks (including me) routinely "saucered 'n blowed" their coffee to cool it down. (You poured as much coffee into the saucer as it would hold, blew across it several times then drank it from the saucer).

Coffee ranked right up there with flour as one of the few store-bought staples. During the Civil War, the coffee supply quickly dried up and, according to a common tale, folks resorted to corn as a substitute. The corn would be parched until it was black, then ground and boiled. Apparently its main resemblance to coffee was that it produced a black beverage.

Although some folks disapproved, in many cases the whole family drank coffee. As far back as I can remember, Mama or Grandma or somebody "seasoned" some for me every morning. They'd put about two or three tablespoons of hot coffee in a glass, then fill it to the brim with sweet milk and sugar.

Breakfast was a big meal, but even so it would have worn off by noon. In the olden days, and even now to some extent, you ate dinner at noon and supper along about late "evening" (that is, late afternoon). Lunch, if the word was ever used at all, was what you packed to take with you to school or to work.

After the woman of the house had milked, fixed breakfast, and cleaned up afterward, she spent the rest of the morning getting dinner ready. In summer, she'd first take a big bucket or basket out and gather a batch of whatever the garden and the pea and corn patches were producing. Then, back in the house she'd stoke up the cook stove and get down to business.

She'd slice the kernels off "roast'nears" (roasting ears, corn grown for the table and not for the livestock) and fix creamed corn in a big skillet, shell and cook up a big pot of black-eyed peas or butterbeans seasoned with a slab of pork fat, and cook some "string beans" the same way. There'd be squash and fresh cucumbers and tomatoes and, of course, "milk" and a big pone of corn bread. Since kitchen counters were scarcer in the Piney Woods than light bread, she did all this peeling and shelling and slicing on a "cook table" about the size of a card table. Similarly, since there was no indoor plumbing, somebody — a young-un, if possible — had to run out to the well several times to fetch a bucket of water. After all this, when she finally "got dinner in the oven," she could sit down and rest a little while.

Then there's okra, which I'm sure that snooty dentist in Lufkin would never, ever, have planted in his garden. Like cornbread, it got packed into our cultural baggage way back yonder. It's a native of Africa and was introduced into the New World by slaves who managed to bring a few seeds with them. Along with its "first cousins," cotton, hollyhocks, hibiscus, althea, and bindweed, it's a member of the Malva family. Okra seed, which are about the size of BBs, contain more protein than just about anything else in the plant kingdom. So in a sense it's sort of like broccoli; it's good for you but some people can't stand it, mostly because the inside of the okra pod contains a clear gelatin-like coating that can be gooey. But okra has a taste all its own which okra lovers find almost addictive. When cooked right — either battered and fried or in soups — the gelatin gets absorbed. If you're still okra-squeamish, try slicing some into about quarter-inch discs, battering them — tempura batter works fine — and frying them wok style.

We seldom had meat in the summer. In the days before refrigerators and freezers, folks made it a point to eat it all before the Texas summer set in. Also, since chickens were allowed to run loose around the place, and since chickens scratch up and eat all sorts of unspeakable things, you didn't just run out and grab up one to have for dinner. Instead, an old rooster or a hen that had quit laying would be penned up early in the week, then fed grain to "flush" out its system by Sunday dinner. Very occasionally there'd be squirrel if somebody had shot one, or fish. When we caught perch in the creek from time to time, Grandma would pack them in salt to preserve them till the next meal (even breakfast!), then batter them in corn meal and fry them.

Folks used to say, "we eat what we can, and what we can't eat, we can." Actually, enough was planted in spring to provide for both summer and winter. So we'd prepare for winter meals on summer days by "putting up" (that is, canning) hundreds of fruit jars (not cans) of vittles. But even with all this bounty from summer, winter dinners were different. For one thing, there was plenty of meat.

A hog destined for the table would be penned up and fed corn for a week or so. Then one day when the sun rose over frosty fields and skim ice formed on the puddles, hog killin' time would be declared. (Remember, those were the days before refrigeration.) From start to finish, this operation took all day. By late "evening," that is, afternoon, the hams, loins, slabs of bacon, and sausage meat would be hanging in the smokehouse over smoldering coals, preferably of hickory wood.

The number of hogs ending up on the table depended on how many mouths there were to feed. Since pork was a mainstay at almost every winter meal, it took at least two or three. Also, besides providing sausage for breakfast and pork or ham for dinner and supper, as much pork as possible was cut up into strips, parboiled, and canned.

In summer, folks planted sweet potatoes, which they harvested in the fall and stored in a "potato house," usually a sort of "throwed-together-looking" shed that nevertheless stayed cool and dry. This could provide the family with about a two-month supply of sweet potatoes. To bake sweet potatoes, all you have to do is wash them, slather them with cooking oil, and throw them in the oven; don't ever poke holes in them unless you look forward to syrupy eruptions. They're also good peeled, sliced, and fried, (like French fries).

Except during the very coldest months (usually January and February) there would be mustard greens, turnips and turnip greens, and (yes) collards. "Regular" potatoes, called Irish potatoes to distinguish them from sweet potatoes, were planted in late winter. They were harvested a couple of months later as "new potatoes," that is, the red-colored ones between the size of a golf ball and a tennis ball. These often replaced the depleted supply of sweet potatoes in the potato house.

Something easy to fix or leftovers were served for supper throughout the year. Tough as the woman of the house was, she was plumb tuckered out by this time of day. Except in winter when its heat was welcome, firing up the cook stove for supper was avoided, so leftovers were usually eaten cold (nobody seemed to object). Often, in winter, soup that had been prepared and canned during the summer, was heated up, and folks crumbled cold corn bread into it.

Lunch, as noted above, was something you took with you when you couldn't eat dinner at home. Second, or third or fourth, time around, syrup buckets served as lunch pails. A typical lunch almost always contained cold biscuits and syrup. In winter it would include a cold baked sweet potato. At any time during the year, any leftovers from fried eggs to drumsticks were packed into the syrup bucket. Since there were no plastic baggies in those days, nor even wax paper out in the Piney Woods, I imagine that those lunches resembled syrup-bucket-sized Sloppy Joes.

In about the early 1950s, when folks in the backwoods got electricity, they called it "getting the lights" and used it only for a few bare bulbs hung by their wires from the ceiling. Then first one and then another family got a refrigerator, and soon everybody had one. Early on it was more of a luxury item than a labor-saving appliance. With it, folks could have iced tea every day in the summer rather than only for a few days after the iceman had been by, and they soon learned to make an ice-creamlike concoction and freeze it in an ice-cube tray.

Jim and Nannie were the first family in Oak Flat to get a refrigerator. A neighbor lady went over to see them and their newfangled machine, and the first thing she saw were pots and pans and buckets filled with ice cubes sitting around all over the place. Nannie told her, "When you leave, take all the ice with you that you can. This new ice box is making it faster than we can use it."

Folks who live out in the boondocks aren't referred to as "country hicks" much anymore, but in the olden days that was meant, and taken, as an insult. We "country hicks" could counter by calling our urban brethren "city dudes," but that never sounded insulting enough to provide much satisfaction. When we really wanted to brand somebody as deficient in common sense or just plain ignorant, we would say that he (or she) would starve to death in the country. And while folks did have to know or learn such things as when the churning had turned, anyone able to put up with the hard work could count on vittles a plenty. Kitchen is closed.

15

STEP-INS AND DUDS

In the Piney Woods, when you needed something you didn't have, somebody would usually say, "Well, you'll just have to do like they do across the river." Even if you'd heard this expression a hundred times, you were supposed to ask, "What's that?" And the answer would be "Do without." Until well into the 1900s, Piney Woods folks did like they do across the river day in and day out, especially when it came to store-bought clothes.

Elias Howe patented the sewing machine in 1846, but the idea of one had been around since at least 1834 when a Frenchman devised a "stitching machine." I.M. Singer improved on Howe's design and, by the time of the Civil War, households all over the country had treadle-operated "Singers." Before that, everything — from clothes to quilts to Betsy Ross's flag — was hand stitched, either by the females of the house, in sweatshop clothing factories, or by swanky tailors and dressmakers. (Ben Franklin's earlier invention of bifocal glasses undoubtedly improved the quality of hand stitchery.)

Our female predecessors certainly sewed a lot, but compared to cooking and canning, it was easy work. Also, many women (and girls) enjoyed sewing; for one thing, it gave them a chance to sit down. But probably more to the point, since everybody's wardrobe was skimpy, a dab of sewing went a long way. To look into these skimpy wardrobes, let's start from the inside out and begin with underwear.

Lots of folks didn't bother much with underwear, but I can't swear to that since I never went around asking them what kind of underwear they had on. I do know that boobs greatly outnumbered bras. And I do know of at least one man who never — well, almost never — wore underwear.

We had two Uncle Buds, and this story is about Uncle Bud Elliot (Aunt Virgie's husband and thus Grandpa's brother-in-law). Unlike a lot of his Piney Woods cohorts, Uncle Bud Elliot took pride in doing things right. He was more of a rancher than a farmer, and he and Aunt Virgie had a pretty big spread that actually made money. He kept up with all the new trends in agriculture and had a knack for deciding which ones made sense. One morning as he and Aunt Virgie were getting dressed, she noticed that he was putting on underwear. She thought this was strange and when she asked him why, he answered, "Well, the Ag Agent's coming today, ain't he?"

Nearly all of everyone's undies, from women's petticoats and camisoles and men's undershirts to everyone's drawers, were homemade of white cotton. Women did wear petticoats or camisoles, and men wore undershirts at least to church, but drawers — and later "step-ins," that is, women's store-bought panties — were often optional. (Once, somebody on the way to town stopped by and asked Grandma if she wanted to go along. She answered, "Yes, wait a minute while I go put on my step-ins.")

"Hosiery" was store-bought and consisted of a few pairs of men's socks and women's "stockings" (what we now call hose). Women might have a pair of silk stockings stashed back for funerals and such (rayon and nylon hose didn't exist until around World War II) but, day in, day out, year round, they wore thick, flesh-colored cotton stockings. They cinched these up above the knee with either garters or, more often, by rolling the top of the stocking into a tight loop then tucking the loop back under itself (sort of like you would wrap and tuck a towel if the pizza man arrived when you were in the shower).

As the day wore on these loops sometimes came loose, then the stockings would slip down and bunch up around the woman's ankles. Most women would then re-cinch them, but those with a more devil-may-care attitude just let them stay drooped. These rolls of flesh colored stockings made the woman look as if she'd developed a severe case of ankle fat. This had to be more comfortable, though, because holding up stockings with either garters or loops amounted to about the same thing as having tourniquets around both lower thighs.

Most women made a beeline to undo their stockings the minute they'd washed the supper dishes. If they'd received a pair of bedroom slippers from some thoughtful soul for Christmas, they'd put them on. But bedroom slippers were about as scarce as store- bought drawers, so they'd either keep on their shoes and drooping stockings or else pad around barefooted. In any case, to keep from depositing foot dirt on the sheets, everybody was expected to wash their feet (in the wash basin) before going to bed. Only those who also probably ate rabbit and clabber went to bed with dirty feet.

Speaking of tourniquets, I suppose a woman or two around the settlement had a corset. A lot of women in town certainly did, but a corset on a country woman would have made about as much sense as bells on a rake. There were a few fat people here and there, including a few men, but I don't recall any that we would now call obese. Besides, women from middle age (around 40) on were expected to be stout. I guess it helped if they had some weight to throw around when milking a stubborn cow.

In the olden days, men slept in long nightshirts, and women in nightgowns, both easy to make at home. Pajamas were not unheard of, but sewing up a pair involved more detail than country women wanted to put up with.

One Christmas season an elderly "maiden lady" did decide she'd make pajamas for her kinfolks, so she carefully sewed and gift-wrapped a bunch. When the family opened the presents, they found she'd made them all from the same pattern. Those for the men lacked even a hint of a fly!

Before we move on to the "outer wear" department, one last item of what can loosely be called "intimate apparel" bears noting. Just as we all know that astronauts have to "go to the bathroom" but NASA never tells us how they manage it, we know, if we've ever thought about it, that women in the olden days had something that passed for sanitary napkins. It's obvious that old rags served the purpose. Yet in all the history books and articles I'm aware of, the subject is never mentioned. We can sort of understand what it took for our female predecessors to milk a cow on a frosty morning or help thin the corn or pick cotton, but I don't think we can begin to imagine how they coped, as they put it, "saddled up."

Now, over into the outer wear department. I've always heard that Texans can stand the hot summers because our blood has thinned. If true, this explains why we chill to the bone when it gets cold. And while it seldom snows in the Piney Woods, it does get cold enough to freeze the horns off a billy goat several times each winter, especially when a Blue Norther blows in.

Blue Northers originate in northern Canada, roar through the U.S. Great Plains, then cut a wide swath through Texas. When a Blue Norther hits, the temperature can drop from a balmy 70 or 80 degrees to freezing in a matter of minutes. (The story is told about a man who, on a warm winter day, got a drink from the water bucket on the front porch. As he was tossing out into the yard the half a dipper full he didn't drink, the cat wandered by. At that very moment, a Blue Norther hit, froze the water he'd flung out, and the chunk of ice smacked the cat on the head.)

To cope with the Blue Northers, and even the plain old ordinary norther, folks did not do like they do across the river, but rather invested in a decent wardrobe of warmies. In winter, most men wore BVD's ("union suits"); women would wear an old sweater between their petticoat and dress. In one of John Brown's Civil War letters to Granny Hutch, he asked her to make and send him a jacket. But, by the end of the 1800s, if not before, except for cases like Dolly Parton sings about in "Coat of Many Colors," folks bought their winter duds at a mercantile store, or more likely, through the Sears and Roebuck catalog.

This included jackets and coats, women's and girl's sweaters, and men's jumpers (made of blue denim and lined with flannel; what today is called a "chore jacket"). A few scarves and pairs of gloves rounded out a family's "paid for" winter necessities. Since most Piney Woods houses lacked even a semblance of a closet, any of these duds that couldn't be hung on a peg or nail were either kept in a chifforobe (that is, a small armoire) or, if they could be folded, in a trunk.

For special occasions, a set of clothes for each family member was also stored in the chifforobe. These were not for "Sunday go to meeting," when folks' newest or best everyday clothes sufficed, but rather for funerals or for picture taking by a photographer. Each female had a dress, often homemade, of better material than everyday cotton. Men usually had a store-bought white shirt and a pair of trousers. Men also had a handful of ties, which they might not wear for years even though they usually got at least one for Christmas. The original "giver" paid maybe a quarter for a tie, but many that hadn't been worn were re-wrapped and given to someone else the following Christmas. (One year, the original giver received a tie he had previously given to someone else.)

Day in and day out, women wore cotton shirtwaist or "Mother Hubbard" style dresses. The skirt part came down well below the knees, the upper part was long sleeved and buttoned up to the neck. Except for being made of different colors and prints, just about every female's dresses looked like a cookie-cutter version of everyone else's. And indeed, women would borrow someone else's store-bought pattern and "duplicate" it on old newspaper. Sometimes someone would have a pattern with some flourish such as puffed sleeves or a yoked skirt, and such a pattern would soon make the rounds of the settlement.

Along with these dresses, women also wore homemade sunbonnets (now sometimes called "prairie bonnets"). The Mother Hubbard dresses and sunbonnets certainly served modesty purposes, but also kept the wearer from getting a suntan. Pale skin, and the paler the better, was a status symbol. It meant that the woman was a "lady" who didn't have to toil in the field, no matter that she helped pick cotton in the summer and such. In fact, that is where the term "red neck" comes from. It originated in Southern plantation country to refer to poor whites who had to work in someone else's fields stooped over all day so that their necks got sunburned. I never even heard the term until I was in college when a student or two from the Deep South would use it to mean "white trash." Now, you're a redneck if _____ (you can fill in the blank).

Men's everyday clothes had a dab more variety than women's, and they were all store-bought. A lot of men wore overalls, mostly of blue denim but sometimes black and white striped. Others wore khaki britches or, as Grandpa did, blue denim dungarees. (Levi's date back to the California Gold Rush in the mid 1800s, but they didn't make it to the Piney Woods for about another hundred years.) Men wore long-sleeved cotton work shirts in summer, and flannel ones in the winter. The only thing they wore even remotely "Western" was hats — straw in summer and felt in winter. These were shaped like today's "cowboy" hats, but they didn't have the high "ten-gallon" crowns and extra wide brims. Men also always kept a bandana handy for wiping sweat, but more important, to tie around their necks so they wouldn't get sunburned.

A few men had boots, certainly not the "cowboy" kind, but rather the Teddy Roosevelt lace-up kind. Most, though, wore high-top leather brogans summer and winter. Women wore lace-up oxfords with what we would call a "walking heel." And recall that young'uns went barefoot just about all the time from early spring until the ground started getting frosty in November. Almost nobody — man, woman, or child — had more than two pairs of shoes, one pair for everyday, and another for Sunday-go-to-meeting and special occasions.

Folks treated their shoes as carefully as if they were the family jewels, which, in a sense they were. (Except for wedding bands, and these were optional, most folks had so little jewelry that they didn't need a jewelry box to keep it in.) In the olden days, a family might gross about a dollar a day, while a pair of shoes could cost several bucks. Keeping the entire family shod, which could include shoes for six, seven, or even 12 young'uns, could run up a tab of $30 or more or, in other words, at least a month's work (equivalent to about what we would spend today on a diamond bracelet).

Skimpy wardrobes did have a positive side. It meant fewer dirty duds to mess with on washday. I've heard tales from other climes about how country folks heated wash water on the kitchen stove in big, oblong copper tubs. Well, sir, that's not how it was done in the Piney Woods. Folks washed in a big three-legged, cast-iron wash pot (actually more of a cauldron), which held about ten gallons of water. Since its legs were stubby, it sat only a few inches above the ground, just high enough to get a roaring fire going under and around it. Getting ready to wash would probably wear out today's most ardent jogger.

First you toted firewood and water from the well to the wash pot (located out behind the house somewhere). It took about an hour for the water to boil, but in the meantime you toted more water to fill a handy washtub, in which you lathered everything with lye soap and scrubbed each garment on a washboard. Then you plopped the whole batch of sudsy clothes into the wash pot and agitated them up and down with a broom-handle-sized stick. Next you lifted the steaming duds over into the handy washtub, now refilled with rinse water (more water to tote). Finally, you wrung them out, which took a strong arm, especially with the overalls.

All this was at least a two-phase operation because you did the "dainty" light coloreds first, then repeated the process for the really grimy work clothes. I won't even go into hanging everything out to dry and then ironing the next day (with flat irons heated on the kitchen stove) because just thinking about all this has tuckered me plumb out. Suffice it to say that women, and whatever young'uns they could collar, did very little on washday besides wash.

(The tale is told on a new bride who hated washday so much that she sneaked the dirty clothes out into the woods and burned them up. Her husband soon found out why she had to buy new duds so often.)

An old saying allows as how early Texas was fine for men and dogs, but hell on women and horses. And, with all the cooking, canning, sewing, washing, and such, Piney Woods women probably had a rougher life than horses. But they went about their work efficiently and, to paraphrase an author who was popular in the 1960s but has now faded into obscurity, "with the heartrending efficiency of the poor all over the world." And they simplified any and everything possible, including peeing.

I've heard some of today's female campers and hikers bemoan the fact that when men have to pee they can just go behind the nearest bush, and zip zap they're through. Females, on the other hand, have to find a secluded spot where they won't moon a passerby, undo their clothes, squat, and hope they won't pee on their feet. Early Piney Woods women didn't have these problems because they also peed standing up. They stood spraddle-legged, pulled their skirt away from their legs, and zip zap they were through. (This is one reason why drawers or step-ins were optional.) They'd stand real still, and with their long skirts they didn't even have to go behind a bush, although they did step a little ways away from any menfolks.

I've seen Grandma and Grandma Wade and a few other old timers, that is, those born in the 1800s do this, but women born after the 1900s did not "practice this custom" that I know of. When I once told a non-Texas-born friend about this, she didn't believe me. She later went on a visit to Grandma's with me, and we all walked down to see the creek. Sure enough, my friend got to witness the "custom" first hand. (Maybe today's female campers and hikers should wear long skirts; step-ins optional.)

16

Lillian Leaves the Nest

The year 1921 marks three "firsts" for Lillian. The "fo'mst first," of course, was becoming a college girl at Sam Houston Normal College, now Sam Houston State University, in Huntsville, Texas, the same school where, 22 years earlier, her fourth cousin John F. Renfro 2 had graduated at age 33. Second, prior to going off to college, Lillian had never traveled beyond the 15 miles to Lufkin except for an occasional 35-mile-or-so trip to visit kinfolks around Nacogdoches or San Augustine. Now, at age 18, she would be a good 100 miles from Oak Flat. The third "first" is just as noteworthy: for the first time in her life she would live in a building with indoor plumbing.

In the late 1800s and early 1900s "normal colleges" flourished all over the U.S. in order to meet the increasing need for schoolteachers. High school graduates who finished a two-year normal college program could get a teaching credential; then, to keep it renewed, most states (including Texas) required the "new" teachers to periodically take additional college courses.

I doubt that the normal-college curriculum included any courses in educational psychology or early childhood development or the like. Instead, since one- and two-room schoolhouses still dotted the hinterlands, it concentrated on a well rounded array of subjects so the teachers could jump not only from one subject to another but also from the first- to eighth-grade levels (that is, so no child would be left behind). It was, in fact, the kind of background you'd want if you had a passel of young'uns you planned to home- school.

I know neither how Lillian traveled to Huntsville nor how she managed to pay college expenses. By then she could have gotten there by bus or even train; either could have added more than 50 miles to the trip if she'd had to change connections in Houston. Or, several families around Huntington owned cars (but not yet Grandpa and Grandma), so maybe somebody drove her, although in those days folks would undertake that long of a trip only with great trepidation.

LILLIAN RUSSELL AT COLLEGE

As to the finances, Lillian might have saved a few dollars she earned by picking cotton. Back then when folks could spare the time from their own crops, they could earn a quarter here and a quarter there helping their neighbors pick cotton. Folks got paid a few cents per pound for what they picked, and a hundred pounds per day was considered really good. Some stalwart souls could pick a bale a day, hence the old song:

> "Jump down, spin around, pick a bale of cotton;
> Jump down, spin around, pick a bale a day."

(Not "Pick a bale of hay," as it's sometimes sung.) Lillian once said that she'd been a good cotton picker but couldn't manage a bale a day.

A more sizeable sum probably came from the old Piney Woods custom of designating a newly born calf or pig as belonging to one of the family's young'uns or grandchillurn. I often heard Grandpa refer to a calf or hog as "That one's Billie Jo's" or whoever's. The animal wasn't raised by the young'un like today's kids raise a calf or hog for a 4-H or Future Farmers project (Grandpa called that organization the "Farture Fumers."). Rather, it was raised and tended to as part of the family's herd then, when it was sold, the money went to cover the designated young'un's needs.

At any rate, Lillian got to Huntsville and finished the required two years. Both Prohibition and the Flapper era had gotten underway but, despite some old photos showing her with bobbed hair and wearing a flapperish-looking dress, she was no flapper. Most of the trappings of modernity were in place, so she probably went to a picture show now and then, maybe even flicks with Charlie Chaplin, and heard some tunes by Irving Berlin. She probably even knew that some young women in way off cities drank "cocktails." But, if there had been a speakeasy around Huntsville, she would never, ever have darkened its door.

LILLIAN RUSSELL AS A YOUNG "FLAPPER"

For one thing, the Dean of Women would surely have heard about it and expelled her. But more important, Lillian had grown up hearing the virtuous preach about the virtues of being virtuous. She had also long been exposed to the prevailing certainty that you would become a slobbering drunkard if so much as a single drop of liquor crossed your lips. And besides, her peers didn't pressure her to "try out" a cocktail or slip off and see what went on inside a roadhouse. Most of her fellow students had grown up in small farming communities under almost exactly the same conditions as Lillian had.

She lived in a home-style dormitory owned and operated by a Mr. and Mrs. Hare. The "Hare House," as it was called, had either two stories or one story with high ceilings (a common way before air conditioning of keeping rooms on the cooler side). The large building, along with its spacious front porch, was neatly painted white.

Going home on weekends was not an option in those days; thus Lillian apparently went back to Oak Flat only over Christmas holidays. So she spent many a night and ate many a meal at the Hare House. She was happy there except for maybe a low spell now and then that wouldn't have warranted pecking out "Carry Me Back to Old Virginie." An old photo shows 17 young women with Mr. and Mrs. Hare standing at one end of the group. The inscription in Lillian's handwriting on the photo states: "I shall never forget these dear people: The Hare Family."

Besides her "family" at the Hare House, "Diddie," as she was now nicknamed, made many close friends with other classmates. Throughout her two years of college, she continued to collect entries in the memory book that she started just before leaving Oak Flat. Most autograph books I've seen (or tried to keep myself) have entries on the first handful of sheets followed by a bunch of blank pages. But Lillian filled hers all the way to the back cover.

When Lillian's friends signed their entries in her Memory Book, they also carefully spelled out the name of their hometowns. Some towns, like Rusk and Henderson were (and are) fairly sizeable, but most are about as well known as Oak Flat and Huntington. They include several entries by students from Glenfawn and others from Shiro, Pine Hill, and Mayflower. The entries range from pledges of lasting remembrance to the just plain countrified. For instance:

> "I shall always remember you by our Thanksgiving dinner which we had at the Hare House.'

"When you get married and your husband gets cross,
    give him a dose of pepper sauce."

"When to this page you chance to turn, If the milk has clabbered, you
    had better go churn."

In later years Lillian never talked about her classes, but judging from several Memory Book entries, they included some pretty solid subjects, such as:

"Remember the happy school days at S.H.N.C. And
    remember me as one of your classmates in 250 Physics."

"Dearest Diddie: I wish you a long and happy life but a
    sudden death. Remember 209 Reading."

Her Spanish teacher wrote a page-long entry in a Spanish that's way beyond my Tex-Mex vocabulary to translate. I did figure out that it ended by wishing Lillian a bed of roses. I still have her Spanish textbook, Curso Practico de Español para Principiantes, copyright 1919. It starts off pretty elementary then dives right into verb endings, tenses for all the pronouns, and such.

The largest number of entries, though, indicate that the young minds were (surprise!) much occupied with marriage. A few on the lighter side of this subject include:

"As sure as comes your wedding day; a broom to you
    I'll send;
In sunshine use the brushy part; in storm the other end."

"Remember me early, remember me late;
For God's sake remember me on your wedding day
And send me a piece of cake.
    (Also remember me as a member of the Hare House family)"

"Long may you live, happy may you be,
    remember when you marry, you are never again free."

I think Lillian was of two minds when it came to marriage. Maybe the above entry reflected her sentiments. Or, if you'll recall, she had made up her mind not to go back to a life of picking cotton and milking cows, so never became enamored of any farm boy back around Huntington. She didn't want to become an old maid either, but she would not marry just anybody to avoid that fate. Instead, she'd wait for "her Prince to come," whenever that might be. That wait seemed over at least once during her college years.

A photo now long gone was once pasted on a page of Lillian's Memory Book. The page is now otherwise empty except for the words "My first beau" in Lillian's handwriting beneath the imprint of the dried paste. We know nothing more about the young man or about why the photo got removed. A couple of other entries may be related, but we don't know whether they refer to the same beau:

"Don't forget that the apple tree never bears fruit until it blooms. I wish you the best of luck with your friend."

"We all know that you and Molia are the life of this crowd. I hope that you'll get that Youngblood, and if a tongue can get him, you will."

Despite being the life of the crowd or having a quick-witted tongue, her college courtship(s) did not pan out. So, at age 20, Miss Russell returned home to join the ranks of our several other teacher kinfolks. Maybe she'd stay "Miss Russell" (or "Miss Lillian," as young female teachers were often called back then) or maybe she'd become Mrs. Something or Another some day. For now, though, she was back to living in unpainted, unplumbed houses, but "Aye God" she had traded in the milk bucket and cotton sack for a blackboard pointer.

Over the following years Miss Lillian taught at various one- and two-room schoolhouses out in the Piney Woods. When she was within commuting distance, such as when she taught at Oak Flat or Ora (down the road a piece from Oak Flat) she lived at home. She taught at Etoile (across the Angelina River from Huntington) where she boarded at another unpainted, unplumbed farmhouse. She taught at Etoile the longest of all her teaching jobs and always looked back at those days and her friends there nostalgically. She and another teacher, Lita, shared "duties" at a two-room schoolhouse, I think at Etoile, and became lifelong friends. I remember that Lita was always there through ups and downs, and that the two always found something to laugh about.

Lillian paid for her upkeep wherever she lived, and even when not living at home she helped out the Russell family as much as she could. In order to keep up her teaching credential she also had to stash enough back to take summer college courses from time to time.

One summer she went to Stephen F. Austin College (now a State University) in Nacogdoches; another summer to Southwest Texas College (also now a State University) in San Marcos in the Texas Hill Country. Maybe Nacogdoches was too close to home to be special because she never talked about it much. San Marcos, on the other hand, is around 200 miles from Lufkin in a completely different natural setting. For Lillian, spending a summer in college there was about like being a foreign exchange student. She often recollected how the clear water in the rivers and streams there flowed over rocky bottoms and formed pools almost too cold to swim in.

A lot of what Lillian and her fellow teachers drilled into their students' heads back in those years was changing as they taught it. Certain periods in history are marked by bursts of creativity. This includes the decade of the 1920s. The arts, sciences, and industry soared. At the same time, heads of state, diplomats, and politicians of all stripes invented new forms of government and shuffled borders around. Many effects, both good and bad, of all of this are with us to this very day.

LILLIAN RUSSELL'S CLASS AT A TWO ROOM SCHOOL HOUSE, CIRCA 1920S

LILLIAN RUSSELL (TOP R) AND CO-TEACHERS AT A TWO ROOM SCHOOL HOUSE

A lot of these world-changing and world-shrinking developments were too complicated for most folks, even those beyond the Piney Woods, to understand or even care about. For instance, during the decade of the 1920s, researchers in physics and chemistry opened up the world of the atom.

Lillian's college course in physics probably did not cover electrons, atomic nuclei, and such. Even if it did she wouldn't have taught about it in a two-room schoolhouse. But the basic insides of the atom, as well as cosmic rays, were discovered. The Earth's magnetic field was analyzed, as was the behavior of X-rays. And the list goes on and on. All this, of course, later led to the atom bomb, nuclear power, CAT (Computerized Axial Tomography) scans, MRI's (Magnetic Resonance Imaging), lasers, electricity from solar panels, and all kinds of advances in electronics, optics, astronomy, etc, etc.

Meanwhile inventors and engineers were just as prolific as their scientific brethren. A patent for the iconoscope (that is, the TV picture tube) was applied for in 1924. A year later, recognizable human features were transmitted during a television demonstration. Color TV was demonstrated in 1928, and a station in Schenectady, New York, broadcast (in black and white) the first regularly scheduled TV. (TV didn't become commonplace, of course, until stations began broadcasting wrestling matches in the 1950s.)

If TV had not yet made it to the masses in the 1920s, the movies had. Those who reached celebrity status (besides Charlie Chaplin) include Cecil B. DeMille, Douglas Fairbanks, D.W. Griffith, and Buster Keaton. And, in 1928, Mickey Mouse. But until the end of the decade, picture shows were silent. A lot of the not so famous were working hard to improve that picture. In 1923 Lee De Forest, who was to electronics what Edison was to electricity, demonstrated a process for sound movies and, by 1929, "talkies" had just flat killed silent movies.

Radio, too, began reaching the masses. The technology had been around for several years, thanks in large part to De Forest. But, due to the lack of broadcasting stations, there wasn't anything to listen to. In the 1920s, regular broadcasts began here and there, beginning with the broadcast of a baseball game in New York in 1921. By 1924, two-and-a-half-million folks in the U.S. owned radios. And if folks couldn't find anything on the radio they wanted to hear, they could listen to the phonograph. In 1926, a new electronic recording technique called the "Electrola" was developed. Two years later, Al Jolson's recording of "Sonny Boy" sold 12 million copies in four weeks.

In fact, the 1920s can be called America's golden age of music. Jazz led the way (except maybe in places like the Piney Woods) as such notables as Louis Armstrong and "Jelly Roll" Morton improvised their way from speakeasies to fame. Musicians such as George Gershwin, Irving Berlin, and Jerome Kern elevated jazz to music hall and Broadway status, with some of their tunes even making it to the hinterlands. Some classical music of the period flunked the test of time (fortunately, I think) but a good bit more seems here to stay. For instance, Aaron Copeland in the U.S. jazzed up old-timey hymns, folk tunes, and such for symphony orchestras. Sibelius in Finland and Wagner in Germany wrote blood-stirring tributes to their homelands.

Art also flourished in the 1920s, mainly in Europe, but a dab in the U.S. Artists such as Picasso, Monet, and Matisse were making a living with their painting; Georgia O'Keefe was getting her start in West Texas and New Mexico.

All this highbrow stuff failed to catch on in the Piney Woods and places like it. For one thing, classical music is difficult to play by ear. And folks' idea of art was something that resembled the scenes of snow-capped mountains or rose bowers printed on the cardboard fans handed out by the mortuary at summer funerals. Folks wanted their culture to be folksy and, sure enough, a homespun humorist from Oklahoma showed up. By 1924, Will Rogers had pretty much roped and joked his way to fame.

As all these things took place on the ground, humankind was fixing to start flying — if not the folksy skies, at least, more or less, the friendly skies. And not just daredevils, either. Lillian never flew in an airplane until her last days. But by the end of the 1920s a lot of people had, including a few Piney Woodsians. Air travel didn't become commonplace until after World War II; in fact, when I was still in pigtails in the late 1930s, I remember running outside to look when we heard an airplane fly over.

By 1926, at least three airlines had begun operation: Aeroflot in the U.S.S.R (1923), British Imperial Airways (1924), and Lufthansa in Germany (1926). Also in 1926, in a demonstration of long-distance flight, Alan Cobham flew from England to South Africa and back. Charles Lindbergh flew non-stop from New York to Paris in the "Spirit of St. Louis" in 1927. The next year Amelia Earhart became the first woman to fly across the Atlantic. In 1926, Robert Goddard in New Mexico successfully launched the first liquid-fueled rocket, but rocket science's time had not yet come.

Dictators, by whatever title they went (or go) by, have strutted around since before Methuselah. More recently, several particularly brutish ones got their start during the decade of the 1920s. In Russia, after one of the worst famines in history plus many battles, the Bolsheviks, headed by Lenin, had gained power. The year before Aeroflot was founded, they officially renamed their landmass the United Soviet Socialist Republic. When Lenin died in 1924, Stalin beat out Trotsky (a feud that had been brewing) to become head of the Communist Party, which meant head of the whole shebang.

Italy, plagued by a sunken economy after World War I, was ruled by a monarchy headed by King Victor Emmanuel III until 1922. In that year, in what we would call a bloodless coup, the Fascist party took over, with Mussolini as Prime Minister. Opposite of the Communist belief that the state exists for its people, the Fascists believed that the people exist only for the glory of the state. Two years later, after the Fascists had gained a majority in Italy's Parliament, Mussolini became head of the whole shebang.

Hitler didn't rise to power in the 1920s, but he was well on his way. Germany, too, had a sunken economy after World War I, and by 1923 it took four million German marks to get one dollar in exchange. It has been said that Germans had to load a whole wheelbarrow full of paper money to go buy a loaf of bread. Add to this a string of chancellors who seemed to have been hired and fired by the week, and, to top it all off, resentful young men who, because of high unemployment, couldn't get hired at anything even for a week. By 1921, Hitler had attracted enough young men to start his own version of the Boy Scouts, that is, the storm troopers, to terrorize political opponents. In 1924, after he and his "troop" started a bloody political riot, Hitler spent eight months in jail where he wrote up his agenda in Mein Kampf. By the next year he had enough followers to reorganize his party, the National Socialist Party, into the Nazi Party. In 1929, as the Nazis had expanded their hate list and gotten bloodier, Hitler appointed Himmler as head of the S.S. Now, Hitler and his henchmen were ready to get down to business.

Some news of these ominous developments reached the Piney Woods, but most folks probably didn't spend much conversation time on them. They were more apt to marvel over such newfangled inventions as the electric razor (1923) even if they didn't have electricity or the permanent wave (1922), which a beauty shop or two in town might be figuring on eventually offering. If they'd heard that the first birth-control center in the U.S. had opened in New York (1923), they would surely have hotly debated its morality. But they would have welcomed the news that Alexander Fleming had discovered penicillin (1928). Country folks wouldn't have cared that Harold Vanderbilt had "invented" the game of contract bridge (1925), although it caught on pretty quickly with high-society folks, particularly throughout the South. High-society folks might likewise have noted that Bobby Jones won just about every golf tournament he entered.

Everyone, from city to town to settlement, knew and cared that the Ford Motor Company was cranking affordable (well, sort of) cars off its assembly line. By the end of the 1920s, one out of about five people in the U.S. owned an automobile. That ratio didn't hold for the less-affluent Piney Woods, though, as would have been apparent by the number of mule or horse drawn wagons parked around town on Saturday. But there were enough automobiles chugging around to occasionally run into each other.

Among all the other things the automobile wrought, it transformed the mate- selection process from courting to dating (although back then it still wasn't proper for a couple to go off to a picture show or something alone). Single men discovered that a car improved their status with the ladies more than a Sears and Roebuck suit. Also, a bachelor with access to a car could woo a lady who lived maybe 35 or 40 miles away.

As you'll recall, Miss Lillian began teaching at age 20. She didn't own a car until several years later but, in her new circle of working adult friends, several folks (mostly young men) did. They all got together and went to picture shows, dances, picnics, and just about anything else that wouldn't besmirch a teacher's reputation and get her (or him) fired. During all this, Miss Lillian had a crush or two on a gentleman or two, and vice versa, but nothing serious. Then a youngish man from, I think, Tyler County joined the group and all that changed.

Miss Lillian, now approaching her mid-twenties, had, if not her first beau, her most serious one. She soon became serious in return, and the two spent as much time together as possible. They were both past the age of puppy love and mature enough to feel sure that they weren't merely infatuated with one another. They made plans for their future together and considered "setting the date." But if Lillian figured they would get married and live happily ever after, she didn't count on a stranger entering the picture.

She met him purely by chance. He was reasonably good looking, but not tall and dark. He would have starved to death in the country, but he had been places she only knew from teaching geography. He wasn't even from Texas. I'm not sure of her "previous" beau's name, but it might have been John. At any rate, I seem to remember hearing that she wrote him a letter that began "Dear John."

17
Fred Graham (1886-1953)

If it had entered my head to ask Daddy if he once considered himself an "adult orphan," he would have answered either "Yep" or "Nope." Probably "Nope." He was friendly enough, but he didn't talk unless he had to. He and I could spend hours together fishing or whatever, and he wouldn't utter more than a few sentences. When asked a question he would answer in as much detail as necessary but no more. He wasn't much of a conversationalist at social gatherings either, although he would add his comments from time to time. I know he did get into technical discussions on the job because his coworkers told me so.

Maybe he was just taciturn, or — more likely — he was severely timid. Mama told me that only in his later years did she realize how timid he was. He and Mama did talk, apparently quite a lot, though I have no idea when. At any rate almost all I know about Daddy's history I learned from Mama. From this I can sketch out Daddy's life in broad outline, but he still remains somewhat a mystery man who eventually made it to the Piney Woods.

The Early Years

Recall that Fred Graham's parents were both full-blooded Scottish. His mother's maiden name was Johnstone, also the name of a town not far from Glasgow in Scotland, and there are still scores of Johnstones in upstate New York around where Dadddy was born. His mother's first name, I think, was Cliomenia. My middle name, Clio, is after some relative of Daddy's, either his mother or maybe an aunt. He had one younger brother who was killed in France in World War I. Daddy said he had lots of other kinfolks whom he lost track of in all his wanderings.

Daddy did tell me two stories about growing up when he was still a boy in Norfolk, Virginia. His father caught him smoking a cigar he had swiped from somewhere. His father told him if he wanted to smoke cigars he would have to learn to do it right, then hitched the horse to the buggy and drove off into the country with Daddy and a big handful of the cigars. As they rode around on the country roads Daddy's father had him smoke one cigar after another right down to a stub. Daddy said that for a while he really imagined he was some kind of "big shot," but then he got sick and threw up. Although he smoked cigarettes all his adult life, he said he could never stand a cigar after that.

The other story Daddy told me about growing up in Norfolk had to do with a hanging, as he was explaining to me the concept and law of double jeopardy. A hanging was scheduled for a convicted criminal, a murderer I think, who everyone agreed was guilty. I asked Daddy if he went to the hanging and he said "Yep." The man was strung up, the trap door sprung open, and the man fell through. But instead of dangling there, the rope broke and he fell to the ground. After much legal debating about stringing him up again, somebody finally ruled that the punishment had been meted out by the first "hanging," and it was unconstitutional to punish someone twice for the same crime.

I had heard somewhere that Daddy graduated from high school at 16, so I asked him one day if that was true and he said "Yep." His mother died while he was still in school, and an aunt from somewhere moved in to take care of the two boys. Daddy said she was over six feet tall and the most domineering woman he had ever seen. (I sometimes wonder if she was the Cliomenia I got my middle name from; I have been told that I share some of her characteristics). Not long after that his father died. Daddy said he put up with the aunt until he finished school then struck out on his own.

One of the first things Daddy did when he left home was to work his way to and from England on a cattle boat. I once asked him if this was true, and he answered (what else?!) "Yep." I have no idea what his job was on the ship, but I do know that he was often kidded about it later on in East Texas where his lack of knowledge about handling livestock had become legendary. He always took the jibes good naturedly about how he managed a boatload of cows.

Daddy then did what all Americans were supposed to do during that period: that is, head west. He didn't do it all in one fell swoop though, but rather in steps from here to there.

The Move West:

I figure Daddy would have started his westward odyssey about 1903 or 1904 when he was around 18. I have a hunch he did not head due west immediately but spent some time working along the Atlantic seaboard first. He always said he had been in every state except Maine so during this period he could have worked in several eastern states. (I thought of Daddy throughout my first visit to Maine). A few pioneering motor cars were around at the time but Daddy most certainly would not have owned one. But thousands of miles of railroad tracks crisscrossed the U.S., and I'll bet he got from point to point by train.

The late 1800s has been called the "century of steam." In fact, the era lasted well into the early 1900s, and by today's standards could also be called the "era of mechanical contraptions." When we think of the age of steam, we tend to visualize steam ships and steam locomotives, but smaller steam boilers (fired by wood, coal, or oil) and steam engines abounded. Just as we plug into an electrical outlet today to get power for pumps, saws, conveyor belts, drills, and the like, for over 100 years the motive force was steam. The steam did not power the tools directly; rather motion produced by the steam engine drove spaghetti mazes of belts and pulleys, gears and clutches. To power a drill press, for instance, a secondary belt drive, maybe with a clutch and gearing, would run from the main belt drive to a sprocket on the drill. Usually the main belts ran overhead so the secondary taps dropped down to the work area. The systems ran fine and were technologically sophisticated. Their main drawback was that they were complicated and the boilers had to be stoked and monitored.

This was the technology of the day when Daddy headed west. He was a mechanical genius (his co-workers have told me that, so I'm not necessarily bragging), and he had no trouble getting jobs. I know that in some towns he worked for the local blacksmith, who contrary to popular perception did not shoe horses (a farrier did that), but rather forged, fashioned and repaired most anything made of metal. I'm pretty certain though that in many places along his way he worked in steam powered shops. I base this mainly on his hearing.

As far back as I can remember he wore a hearing aid and could not hear much without one. Up until the 1940s the main unit was about the size of a hardback novel and contained four D-cell batteries. It was worn in a special shoulder holster, and connected by wire to a large earpiece mounted on a headphone-type steel band that fit over the top of the head.

Under the Black Gum Tree

The technology that allowed the shrinking of hearing aids became available right before World War II, and Daddy was quick to buy one of the new units. At any rate, Daddy always said his hearing was ruined working in boiler rooms, and I'm certain he never worked in a boiler room unless it was on his way west and his jobs while out west.

Daddy apparently stayed and worked for a good while in some places. He told Mama that, in a town in Iowa, he made and saved what, in those days, was a lot of money. Being prudent, he deposited it in the local bank. The bank, however, went belly up. He tried to get it back but to no avail since there was no such thing as the FDIC then. This could very well have happened in 1907 since a nationwide panic caused a run on banks in that year. Daddy also told Mama that, on his migration west, he worked in Detroit (for either General Motors or Ford Motors; I can't remember which). In those days the competition to get motor cars out to the general public would have been fierce. In 1908 General Motors was founded, and Henry Ford produced the first Model T's; then in 1913, Henry Ford developed the assembly line.

The company Daddy worked for powered its automobiles' headlights with a magneto. The other company powered its headlights off the vehicle's electrical system, and Daddy's company was anxious to do likewise. Whichever one Daddy worked for "fired" him, and sent him off to work for the other company to find out exactly how they ran their headlights. Daddy was apparently successful and took back the details to his "first" company. He was, in short, what today we would call an industrial spy.

San Francisco:

I don't know whether it was "San Francisco or bust" or just another stop in his odyssey. I like to imagine that he arrived on a warm summer day with the bay shimmering in the sunshine. The air would have had a cool, minty tang mixed with the scents from the fishing wharves and mud flats. Trams and freight wagons, many of them horse-drawn, would have been clanging their way up and down the narrow streets. Daddy would have been used to the seaside from his days in Norfolk, and to a city's hustle and bustle from living in Detroit. But he probably would not have been familiar with California's aura of excitement that has lasted from the Gold Rush until today.

He was a young man in his early twenties, and the year would have been nineteen-ought-something. There was plenty of work to be had and ambitions waiting to be fulfilled. He was to live there for five years at least, and maybe even eight or ten.

He told Mama he loved San Francisco more than any other place he had ever lived. People were always out and about going places and doing things, and he joined right in. He bought a tuxedo that he wore to fancy balls and banquets. Fishing and hunting were always a big enjoyment in his life, and I suspect he had plenty of opportunities for both. In those days before California became jam packed with people, one could take a train or tram to the outskirts of town and hike into the wilderness.

I know he visited the red-light district. I do not know how often. He told Mama that upon entering the fancier bordellos, the "patron" had to wash his penis in a pan of disinfectant. A gentleman I know, who shall remain anonymous, told me the requirement was still enforced when he went to a posh San Francisco bordello a few years back. He said the container is called the "peter pan."

Daddy probably spent many of his years in San Francisco working in machine shops or factories, and as we have seen, these relied on steam power. One day the shop building caught on fire. The blaze began spreading and would have soon engulfed the building unless the gas supply was shut off. Daddy dashed through the flames to the main gas valve and closed it. Firemen were then able to put out the fire.

Daddy's boss thanked him profusely for saving his business and asked what he could do in return. Daddy replied that he had always wanted to go to college to study engineering but had never had the opportunity. He asked to be allowed to work at night so he could go to college during the day. And that is how Daddy became a mechanical engineer.

Daddy could possibly have been in San Francisco during the 1906 earthquake, but I don't think so. I never heard it so much as mentioned, and if he had been through it I surely would have heard something. Experiencing an earthquake of that magnitude would be about as noteworthy as hearing Gabriel toot his horn. Some relatives have speculated that the fire he helped put out was caused by the earthquake, and maybe it was. But fires in the steam-powered shops of those days were a common hazard and didn't require an earthquake to set them off.

I know Daddy attended the University of California. At that time, German was required for an engineering degree. It was held that the best technological papers and texts were written in Germany and too complex to translate correctly, so engineers had to be able to read them in their original language. Daddy passed every single, solitary requirement for a degree except German. After taking it several times he decided he could never learn German and left college.

Not having a degree because he couldn't pass German was always a bitter pill for Daddy, but it didn't stop him from being an engineer. He later passed the rigorous examination for his professional engineers' registration, which is comparable to a lawyer passing the bar exam. Daddy later liked to point out with gleeful satisfaction that, when the World War came along, the German treatises were translated into English in short order. (Note that up through the 1960s some engineering colleges still required two semesters of German.)

Daddy could have gotten through college in four years, but that's a bare minimum for engineering, and a five-year, full-time course of study has long been common. Engineering students are immersed in math, physics and chemistry, along with history, English, etc., before they can even begin their engineering courses. Upon reaching the upper level, they spend all day in class. Lecture classes take up the entire morning, and Daddy's would have included thermodynamics, hydraulics, the theory and design of steam engines, the principles of pressure vessels and such. The tired engineering students then spend all afternoon in lab work; Daddy's would have included running various types of machinery and taking measurements galore. And then there's homework. With Daddy going to school all day and working nights, it must have been hard to squeeze in time for fancy balls and banquets.

I don't know how long Daddy stayed in San Francisco after he left college. He might have worked in California for a while, or even somewhere else, but his history is blank until it picks up again in the mid-19-teens in Texas. Maybe he moved on because he was disappointed in love. He would have been of a "courting" age. Maybe he tried to go into some business but didn't make it. Or, maybe the booming oil business lured him to Texas.

In Texas:

Shoving hundreds of feet of drill stem, with its attached bit, down into the earth to find oil has always been pretty much like pushing a rope. As the borehole goes deeper, the drill stem writhes and twists, and the bit clogs, dulls, and wears out as it grinds its way through mud, clay, and rock. The couplings and fittings joining the stem sections to one another and to the surface, after running continuously day in and day out, get tired and quit when they're not supposed to. Since the beginning of the oil industry, big bucks have been there to be made for improving all these devices, mechanisms, and equipment. When Daddy arrived in Texas, the young oil industry was wide open to innovations and new inventions.

The earliest of Daddy's jobs in Texas, but maybe not the first, was with Hughes Tool Company, probably in Houston. The company, founded by the father of the flamboyant Howard Hughes, designed and manufactured a wide range of special tools to help the drill stem and bit cut its way down to the oil-bearing strata. (Howard much later took over the company and transformed it into Hughes Aircraft to build the Spruce Goose, helicopters, and such).

Daddy and a coworker, Walter, also an engineer, became close, lifelong friends. Walter was only slightly more talkative that Daddy, so when they got together for visits or to go fishing, they exchanged the news and a few pleasantries then didn't say another word for hours. When it was time to leave, they always told each other what a good time they'd had.

Walter invented some kind of special improved drilling device and wanted to patent it in his name. This led to a dispute when the company insisted on patenting it in its name, which meant the company would get all the royalties. Walter quit and started his own company to manufacture it. His device sold like hotcakes, and Walter became rich. He and his family lived quite comfortably ever after, but they never took on the trappings of the wealthy class. (Since then it has long been common practice that, upon accepting employment, an engineer signs away all patent rights to his or her employer.)

At some point in here, Daddy got married. Mama told me about it in the barest of details, namely: "Fred married a woman from Beaumont, and she committed suicide. He told me it was a case of they couldn't live together and couldn't live without each other." I knew from Mama's way of telling me that it was a deep dark secret, and I was afraid to ask her for any more details.

Oil field equipment was being improved at a breakneck pace in those days, and Walter Trout, Sr. (a different Walter) struck upon an idea for getting in on the act. His foundry in Lufkin manufactured saw mill equipment, and he became convinced he could build a better oil-pumping unit than the clunky wooden ones then in use. It had to be designed first though, and Mr. Trout needed a good engineer for the job. Then, as now, good engineers were scarce. But he did find one: Fred Graham.

Daddy worked for the Lufkin Foundry and Machine Co. for over 20 years, beginning shortly after World War I. Younger engineers were brought in to help, but he did a good bit of the design work on the Lufkin

Fred Graham, fifth from the left, and his co-workers at the Lufkin Foundry (Circa 1932)

pumping unit. Its distinctive features include the "cat head," that dinosaur-head of a looking thing at the front that pushes and pulls the pump rod up and down with a smooth "bumpless" motion, and the counterweights at the back which translate the circular motion of the pump engine into the up and down motion of the cross beam. The basic design of the unit remained unchanged for years. Whenever you see a pumping unit with the word "Lufkin" on the cross beam, which will be every time you are near any oil field from Bahrain to Lubbock to Brunei, think of Fred Graham.

Daddy got married again during this period; probably during his early years at the "Foundry." His wife's parents ran a little neighborhood grocery store in front of their house in Lufkin. I don't know much more about this marriage than about the one to the woman in Beaumont. I do know they got a divorce. Later on, by the time I was only a first grader, I knew none of our family was ever supposed to go to "That Store," even though it was only about four blocks from our house.

Our good nursemaid, Bennie, always took my brothers and me on some kind of outing in the afternoons; a few blocks over to the Coca Cola plant to watch through the big window as the bottles were being filled, or down Raguet Street past the mansions of the wealthy families who had made their money in the sawmill business. One day, unbeknownst, she took us to "That Store" to buy us peppermint sticks.

I can still see the woman behind the counter: she was old, at least to my way of thinking, and had a grim expression. We had barely walked into the store when she said, "You're Fred Graham's children, aren't you?" Bennie, sensing that something was amiss, said, "Yes ma'am," then quickly paid for our peppermints and herded us out the door. Bennie and Mama had a close, friendly relationship, and I'm sure they talked about it when we got home. We never even went in the direction of "That Store" again.

I don't know anything else about the divorce. I have a vague notion the breakup was over money. Daddy made a decent salary for those days, and especially for the countrified environs of Lufkin. In my recollection he was always generous but never interested in money for its own sake. He lived a simple life, and the only luxuries he allowed himself (when he could afford them) were a well-designed automobile, high-quality tools, and good hunting and fishing equipment. It's possible his ex-wife had visions of living in a mansion on Raguet Street, or maybe she just nickel-and-dimed him into debt. I know he firmly believed that debt goeth before a downfall. (It's also possible that he couldn't put up with a grim mother-in-law).

Daddy and his friend Walter visited back and forth often; Walter from Houston and Daddy from wherever he, or we, lived. In about 1928, Walter was visiting Daddy in Lufkin, where the county fair was in full swing. They went to the fair and ran into several teachers from country schools in the area, one of whom Walter knew. After introductions all around, Daddy rode the Ferris wheel with one of them. He asked if he could come visit her. She said, "Yes." Her name was Lillian Russell.

Lillian about the time she met Fred

Fred about the time he met Lillian

18
The Ferris Wheel Ride

From the top of their Ferris wheel ride at the county fair, Fred and Lillian could have looked out at patches of Piney Woods and farms, the water tower off in the distance, and the sprawl of the Foundry's buildings a few blocks from downtown Lufkin. They probably didn't though since they most certainly had eyes only for each other. Besides, the ride they had started together would reach heights none of the fair's clunky "little ole" Ferris wheels ever could.

According to conventional wisdom, however, their ride together should never have gotten off the ground. Fred, at about the same age as Grandma, was almost 17 years old and already out on his own when Lillian was born. He couldn't have milked a cow even if it'd had an udder full of ambrosia. From the outside Lillian could have mistaken a big city museum for the county courthouse. Fred might not even have liked black-eyed peas until he had been taught otherwise, and she never did learn to like steak even slightly pinkish in the middle.

With Fred working at the Foundry and Lillian teaching out in the country, they got together on weekends and wrote to each other in between. I feel kind of sorry for couples today that do their courting via e-mail. They can wrap their virtual love letters in a virtual ribbon, and maybe get gushy about their beloveds' keystrokes the way folks used to gush about the handwritten signatures and the color of the ink and so forth. Certainly couples now can get printouts, and I guess my age is showing, but that strikes me as about as sentimental as a credit-card bill.

I don't know what happened to Lillian's love letters to Fred, but she saved a batch he wrote to her. She did keep them tied up in a nice neat packet, which we still have. None of us has ever read more of them, though, than the first paragraph or so of the first one in the packet. They're so personal and intimate, but romantic rather than sexual, that they make you feel like you've barged into an occupied bathroom and must apologize and shut the door behind you right quick. I never got beyond the first sentence that said something like "I dreamed about you last night and didn't want to wake up." Till this good day I have never read any more.

Their courtship lasted over a year. As independent adults they could have gotten married any time the notion struck them, but Lillian postponed it until the family accepted Fred. Of the three Piney Woods strikes he had against him, his age was a bigger drawback than his divorce or citified ways. She told me that once during their courtship Grandpa said, "That old man can't keep his hands off Lillian." A questionable marriage has never caused anyone in our bunch to be disowned, but it has frayed family ties on several occasions. The family finally did decide that they liked Fred even if he didn't fit their conventional mold.

"Black Friday," the 28th of October, 1929, marked the beginning of the Great Depression when stock markets and, later, banks collapsed all over the U.S. and Europe. Previously wealthy stockbrokers in New York City would soon be out on the streets peddling apples, but Fred and Lillian were far from depressed. On Christmas Eve of that year they tied the knot in a no frills ceremony in the parsonage of the First Christian Church in Lufkin. Several days before that, the pastor had baptized Fred, who had been sprinkled into the Episcopal Church as a young tot. Fred thought that was good enough, but the pastor insisted he be baptized by immersion. Since Fred was in an agreeable mood he didn't argue, but he was never much of a churchgoer. Fred and Lillian honeymooned in Galveston and until by death did they part.

The honeymoon lasted throughout the 23 years of their marriage. Any time Fred saw something he thought Lillian would like, he bought it for her. (My brothers and I still have all these gifts on mantles and shelves and in jewelry boxes.) After Fred's death, Lillian's ex-beau — the one she wrote the Dear John letter to — came a-courting again. She saw him several times then turned him down again. As she once told me, she couldn't imagine crawling into bed with anybody but Fred. Both our parents loved us young'uns, and loved us a lot. But their world did not revolve around us. As one of my brothers put it, we were first and foremost biological by-products.

After living in an apartment for several years, Fred and Lillian bought a house. By then the Depression was in full swing, but Fred's job was fairly secure since oil gets pumped even during hard times. Many farming folks in the Piney Woods didn't feel the full effects of the Depression anyway. As Aunt Addie said years later when interviewed by a young whippersnapper reporter, "We were always poor anyway and grew everything we needed to eat, so everything was about as usual for us."

Cash was scarcer than usual, though, so lots of folks did have to scramble to make a buck or two. Menfolks who were strong enough made a dollar a day splitting logs for railroad ties. Country folks selling fruit and vegetables door to door in town could depend on making some loose change. Little boys, especially, in their best overalls with the familiar smell of homemade lye soap, lugged buckets of produce up one street and down the next.

One day along about this time I invented a new but short-lived game. While playing on the front porch I discovered it was fun to ring the doorbell then run and hide behind the big wax-leaf ligustrum bush before Mama rushed to answer the door. I pulled this stunt several times before she caught me red-handed and threatened to "blister my butt" if I did it again. I knew she meant it so I sat down behind the ligustrum to think up another game. A few minutes later a little boy came along with two big buckets of blackberries and rang the doorbell. Mama dashed out, snapped a switch off the ligustrum bush, and whupped my butt good and proper. She then noticed the little boy cringing in the corner, probably wondering if he was next. She felt so bad about the whole fracas that she bought every last smidgen of the little boy's berries.

Men with some musical talent and the instruments to go with it found another door-to-door way of making some loose change. They'd put together a little band and stroll around mariachi-like. From time to time a group came down our street along about dusky dark as we sat on the porch after supper. They'd stop for a while at the front doorsteps and play and sing popular tunes. I still remember the tune and first few lines of my favorite:

> Oh Johnny, oh Johnny, how you can love,
> Oh Johnny, oh Johnny, heavens above.
> You make my poor heart jump for joy. . .

Maybe you remember the rest of it. When it was time for the band to move on, Daddy would fish a handful of change out of his pocket to give them.

Hobos came around more often than the "mariachis." Some were no account to start with, but many honest young men, especially those from big cities and dust bowl farms, rode the rails as a last resort. (A friend said her brother rode the rails so the family would have one less mouth to feed.) At least one hobo a week knocked on our back door, and Mama always fixed him a full plate. Since she would never, ever let him into the house, she had him eat on the back stoop and made sure she kept the screen door latched (in those days folks thought the little hook on the screen door was enough to keep out anyone with criminal ideas). After he finished, she boiled a pot of water to sterilize everything he had touched.

My folks occasionally got hit up for more than a plate lunch or some nickels and dimes. Daddy got an out-of-work cousin an entry-level job, as we would now call it, at the Foundry. That part turned out okay, but the young man had several plain no account siblings who then began pestering Mama for paper-money-sized handouts. After a few such "donations," Mama, who knew all about these cousins' shiftless ways, turned off the tap. One of them then went to Daddy's office during working hours asking for a "loan." This made Mama so mad she was about ready to fart a rug. Even the shiftless cousins then got the picture and quit coming around. I'd bet though, that they went around telling everybody they could that Lillian had married Fred and gotten snooty.

Lillian and Fred were certainly not the best-heeled of the contingent in town, but they weren't exactly padding around in bedroom slippers either. They belonged to the country club, and both played golf. She was the more serious about it and placed high in several tournaments. He built a skiff and kept it moored at the club's lake to fish from, often while she played golf. From time to time they bowled, which he especially enjoyed. They both loved to dance.

Lillian belonged to several "ladies groups," including the ladies' fellowship at church. She belonged to the book club and read all the bestsellers. She had our family's passion for gardening and joined the garden club. Then there was the bridge club and baby showers and wedding showers and luncheons, luncheons, luncheons. Back then I thought a luncheon was some mysterious ritual where ladies dressed up and went out to eat asparagus spears on toast.

The asparagus came from a can; I doubt if anyone back then had ever seen a fresh stalk of asparagus. For the toast, white bread was first halved diagonally and the crust trimmed off. Finally the whole shebang was topped with a scoop of white sauce and served on a salad plate. There must have been other things on the menu, but asparagus on toast is all I ever knew about.

This may sound like a hectic schedule but, in those days before TV and Little League and such, I remember many quiet times and fun times. At night in the living room we could have passed for a Thomas Kinkaide picture-perfect family scene. When we young'uns got tired of playing with our toys and games on the floor we would get "sentimental" ("segimental," as I pronounced it) and crawl up into a parent's lap. It did bother me though that Daddy would never get down on the floor to play with us as I knew that my playmates' daddies did. Once when I was being "segimental" in Mama's lap I asked her why he always sat in his chair. She figured this out right off the bat and said, "Just because Fred doesn't get down on the floor with y'all doesn't mean he doesn't love you. He loves you a lot more than all the younger daddies love your playmates."

We took all kinds of trips. For vacation, we always went to Rockport and rented a "tourist cabin" on the beach near Corpus Christi. We swam and fished to our heart's content, but I secretly felt Galveston, where my playmates' families in the well-heeled contingent vacationed, would have been more fun. We went to Houston a time or two a year and stayed in the Cotton Hotel (now long gone) over by Union Station and the old Cotton Exchange. It was not as highfalutin' as the Rice Hotel, which we couldn't afford, but quite respectable, and we often did eat at the Rice Hotel Cafeteria. Mama shopped a lot, sometimes at Foley's, for Christmas presents and school clothes and rounds of shoes for all of us. She also bought "right now presents" for all the young'uns in the connection. I can still see all the packages stacked up in the hotel room.

No matter how much fun other trips were I thought then, and still do, that visiting kinfolks was the most fun of all. We went to see Grandma and Grandpa and others around Huntington just about every Sunday afternoon. Most businesses back then decreed that the work week included Saturday morning, so we often left as soon Daddy got off work and stayed overnight. The road out to Oak Flat wouldn't be paved for many more years, so in rainy weather it could be slippery at best and we sometimes got stuck. Once Grandpa had to come pull us out of a mud hole with his team.

We made longer trips several times a year. We went to see Aunt Cora (Grandma's sister) and her bunch in Shelby County and Aunt Virgie (Grandpa's sister) and her family in Tyler County. One Easter Sunday, we hunted our eggs on the way to Aunt Virgie's. We had left home too early for an egg hunt there, so Mama took our eggs with us. When we stopped at the Neches River bridge, Mama hid our eggs along the riverbank.

At these family visits everyone, except maybe a sourpuss or two or someone whose rheumatism was acting up, laughed and joked, it seemed, nonstop. "New" things had to be checked out too: a new calf, a just-sprouted cornfield, new spokes Grandpa was carving for a wagon wheel. We picked berries or yellow jasmine or wild persimmons in the woods. A young'un or two also usually got into trouble. I got into a patch of stinging nettle once (but only once). Another time we had a hanging.

There was a deep gully in the lane to Grandpa's cornfield that he had built a bridge across. The bank under the bridge had a steep slick of clayish soil that made a perfect slide for young'uns. That is, until my brother Fred got caught between the planks where one had broken off and left a gap. He was sliding down whoopty-do and poked his head up just at the gap. And there he hung in thin air, dangling from his chin and the back of his skull between the planks. Fortunately several folks checking out the corn crop nearby rescued him.

We also visited back and forth with lots of neighbors, friends, and kinfolks in Lufkin. Folks often dropped in and, if it seemed appropriate, sat around the dining room table. They talked about grownup stuff such as goings on around town, whether the farmers' crops looked good, and the WPA and the CCC and such. As the years went by, they talked more and more about the mess in Europe. All this usually bored me so I went on about my business. In the summer of 1940, though, something about the tone of their conversation caused me to hang around and listen. They were arguing, in a polite way, whether to vote for Franklin Roosevelt or Wendell Willkie. I remember, almost verbatim, that one woman said, "Well, I'm going to vote for FDR because he's promised to keep us out of the war, and I believe him."

The following year, on December 7th, we made our usual Sunday-afternoon trip to see Grandma and Grandpa. Except nothing was usual about it. Nobody laughed or joked or even talked very much. I had asked Daddy that morning how long the war would last. He had answered, "Nobody knows. One war lasted over a hundred years."

Grandpa always kept a blacksmithing set-up under a spreading oak tree behind the house. Over the years he had accumulated piles of old scrap metal and even a worn-out Model T. Earlier in '41, a man came through buying junk metal to export to Japan and Grandpa sold him a batch of it. For the rest of his life he regretted selling it and, on that Sunday, he said, "I guess the Japs will melt it all down for bullets and shoot them back at us."

I think these comments pretty well reflect the grownups' state of mind that day. Even though angered and shocked, they sensed that Pearl Harbor augured a long war, and that battles could very well be fought on our home grounds. The events and changes the war did bring about were beyond everyone's imagination. Yet, no matter what else would happen, Lillian's and Fred's magical Ferris wheel ride never faltered.

Lillian and Fred on their honeymoon in Galveston, December 1929

#7 UNDER THE BLACK GUM
THE TRUNK IN THE GARAGE

Some folks still store things or hide them away in their attic. Mostly now, though, everything from memorabilia to junk gets stacked up in the garage. The attic is a much safer place, especially for treasured items. Unlike the ground level garage, the attic is not as apt to be invaded by bugs, rain runoff, or curious young'uns.

Our house in Lufkin had a rather inaccessible attic, so part of the garage served for both a workshop and storage. Tools and spare parts of all varieties filled Daddy's workshop portion, and as you might expect from an engineer, they were organized in hardware-store fashion. A less well-organized jumble of odds and ends filled most of the storage portion. The trunk sat in an open space away from the jumble.

Probably from about the time I learned to walk and talk, I knew without being told not to ever mess with any of Daddy's stuff. I spent a lot of time with him in the garage, though, and he often let me "help" him fix something. The jumble had some good places to scrunch behind when we young'uns played "hide'n go seek," but I don't recall paying much attention to it otherwise. That is, until one day when the grownups got busy with grownup affairs and I got bored.

I ventured out into the garage alone and prowled around some. Then my curiosity about the trunk got the best of me. I was old enough, at around six, to know I shouldn't meddle, but young enough to meddle anyhow. So I opened the trunk.

If I had expected to find something like presents hidden away until the next Christmas, I was disappointed. Instead, I found a lot of things I couldn't understand: some silky, skinny flapperish dresses, costume jewelry, a comb and a brush, a few books. A sealed envelope contained a lock of light brown hair. Then I spied an old but unopened package of chewing gum. I didn't recognize its faded wrapper, but I knew it was chewing gum.

I must have been a spoiled brat back then. I wouldn't go to bed until

Daddy gave me a stick of gum (If someone forgot to take it out of my mouth after I had gone to sleep, Mama had to cut it out of my hair the next morning.). I guess that made me feel entitled to chewing gum because I opened the package from the trunk.

All the wrappers and the gum began to crumble, but I got almost a stick's worth and tried to chew it. It wouldn't congeal into a wad in my mouth, so I spit it out. I recall realizing at that point that I had treaded on forbidden ground, so I tried to put everything back together. Most of the lock of hair didn't fit back into its envelope, and the chewing gum package had disintegrated. I'm sure nothing else went back right either.

I don't recall when Mama discovered my trespass. I was with her when she did and figured my butt was about to get whupped for sure. Instead, she didn't fuss at me one bit and began crying. That must have burned the whole episode into my memory because I still look back on it with shame. Only in my later years did I realize I had blundered into some of Mama's sister Winnie's last possessions.

To me now, the trunk symbolizes Aunt Winnie's unfinished life. During her short span she accumulated almost nothing of worldly value to be displayed on a mantle or shelf. Neither did she have some special talent that would have led to great worldly accomplishments. She did have a talent for making people laugh and feel better, and to look forward to being with her. The trunk's contents, then, were like unredeemable tokens to special moments that could have been.

She died at age 24 in the Lufkin Hospital after being sick for several months. It started with a tubal pregnancy and then "blood poisoning" set in. Such problems were not easily diagnosed back then and even harder to treat. Alexander Fleming had discovered penicillin three years earlier, but it took another 15 years to develop it into an antibiotic. Even if it had been available it might not have knocked out whatever was causing the "blood poisoning." Aunt Winnie's survivors included a much-bereaved husband but no children.

A YOUNG AUNT
WINNIE RUSSELL

Aunt Winnie was good looking enough but certainly no beauty. I don't know whether she had a streak of vanity, but she did have at least one bad hair day. In about her sixth or seventh grade class picture she cut her face out of the photograph because she didn't like the way her hair looked. I know she had lots of friends, and I suppose beaux. She was the first of Grandpa's and Grandma's children to marry (Mama and Daddy didn't get married until five years later).

Aunt Winnie, at 18, married Forrest Jackson in 1924. They seemed to have made ends meet all right by Piney Woods standards. She taught school as long as she was able. Forrest taught school and also sold insurance all over the county. For a while they ran an ice house in Lufkin. I gather that their devotion to one another throughout their six-plus years together made up for any financial shortage.

After Aunt Winnie's death Forrest remained deeply devoted to her and visited the cemetery often, some said every few days for a while. He remarried quite a few years later but continued to be a dutiful son-in-law to our side of the family for many more years.

Aunt Winnie died two years before I was born. I feel like I know her, though, but not so much from what I heard, since folks seldom spoke of her. When they did, a sense of her loving and loveable nature came through because, even after she had been gone for years and years, it always seemed as though their grief was still raw.

At some point over the years the trunk and its rather trivial contents disappeared. Likewise, almost all those who would remember her have gone on. I hope there are still some folks around now who, like me, came to love Aunt Winnie through the loss felt by others. I wish I had known her.

WINNIE RUSSELL JACKSON, CIRCA LATE 1920S

19
The Pine Grove

When I was growing up, the Pine Grove always attracted my attention. Located a little ways out from Huntington on the road to Oak Flat, it lacked the rambunctious undergrowth we often scrambled though in the woods. It covered a few acres on a gentle slope overlooking the road. It didn't have a name but I thought of it to myself as the Pine Grove. A stand of mature pines shaded the entire spot and nary a weed poked up through its carpet of pine straw (that is, fallen pine needles). It had the same park-like look as the illustrations of the English forest in my Peter Rabbit books. Every time we drove by it I imagined having a picnic under one of the trees.

I didn't tell anybody about my imagined picnic until one day when Mama's sister Mary went along with us out to Grandma's and Grandpa's. As we passed the Pine Grove I said casually, so it would sound as though it had just occurred to me, that the spot looked like a fine place for a picnic. One morning a while later when I was staying a spell with Aunt Mary and Uncle Kyle, she started fixing lunch right after breakfast. Then she packed it into paper sacks and announced that we were going on a picnic.

A few other young'uns went with us, and we spread our lunch (peanut butter and banana sandwiches, always my favorite) on the pine straw under a tree. We laughed, and Aunt Mary sang a tune or two for us. It was all just as I'd imagined. (Peter Rabbit didn't hippity-hop by, but I didn't expect him to.)

We young'uns were fond of many of our kinfolks (as you may have noticed) but Aunt Mary held a special place in our lives. She was more like one of our buddies, partly because she was young enough to do things and go places with us. At 16 she married Uncle Kyle, and their daughter Billie Jo (their only child) came along the next year. Uncle Kyle sometimes earned a paycheck by driving big bulldozers on the road crew or by being a lookout atop a fire tower for the Forest Service. But he always figured he wasn't working unless he was farming, so he'd periodically quit to raise a crop. To support the family during his farming sprees, Aunt Mary worked at local cafes, and in later years ran the bus station café, then her own ("Mary's Place") in Huntington. Since "food service" and Piney Woods farming ranked at the bottom of the profitable occupation list back then, they were always dirt poor.

Aunt Mary could usually think up some way to have fun on little or no cash. One afternoon as she and I sat out in the yard with two of Billie Jo's pre-school boys, they got bored and started getting "aggervating." So, after getting them simmered down, she told them how to build play-like things out of dirt (that is, like building sand castles at the beach). The boys got busy and, by suppertime, a maze of little boy roads with patted out dirt filling stations wound around the yard. With the boys thus occupied, she said to me, "You know, young'uns don't know how to play unless you tell them how to get started."

Uncle Kyle adored Aunt Mary even if she did tease him unmercifully. He was pretty slow to catch on to a joke or a prank so she had plenty of opportunities to josh around with him. During the war when new agencies seemed to spring up overnight, she wrote him a government-looking letter with some words she had made up and had a friend mail it from Houston. She cited his failures to comply with all kinds of official-sounding regulations and ended by saying, "You are now under the jurisdiction of the Government Punt." Uncle Kyle read the letter over and over, looking more worried each time. Finally he said, "Mary, what in the hell is the Government Punt?"

Once there was a Mom and Pop "recreation spot" on the San Jacinto River just off the highway to Houston. A rustic hand-painted roadway sign scrolled down through its menu of activities, namely:

> Fishing
> Camping
> Picnicking
> Swimming
> Horses

One day on their way to Houston to visit kinfolks, Aunt Mary read this list to Uncle Kyle, who humphed and kept on driving. Aunt Mary then said, "Kyle, turn around and let's go back there. I want to see them swimming horses." He replied, "Aw Mary, they ain't got no swimming horses. That's just a come-on to get you down there to spend money."

Aunt Mary wasn't always full of fun and games, though. She loved

Under the Black Gum Tree

Uncle Kyle and stuck by him, but from time to time she lost her patience and reamed him out good. She could also be flirtatious, which she didn't try to hide from anybody. Uncle Kyle never seemed to let any of this bother him. When I was just a little girl I picked up a good addition to my vocabulary by eavesdropping on a fuss between Mama and Aunt Mary. I don't know what it was all about, but one of them said, "I feel like I've been shit on and kicked for stinking." At some point Aunt Mary said, "Lillian, you'll rue this day." I do not know whether Mama rued the day or not, but the two made their peace pretty quick.

Aunt Mary could also be tough when she had to. One day, when she went out to the chicken house to gather the day's eggs, she spotted a great big ole' chicken snake up in the rafters. She decided right quick that she could kill it only by shooting it, even though she didn't know much about guns. She knew Uncle Kyle kept his shotgun loaded and ran and got it. When she got back to the chicken house, the snake was still stretched out on a rafter under the tin roof. She stood in the doorway, took aim the way she thought she should and pulled the trigger. The blast threw her back several feet, but it had blown the snake to smithereens. It also blew a hole in the tin roof big enough to drop a washtub through!

I don't think Aunt Mary ever became a bona fide member of any church although she attended the Pentecostal Church in an on again, off again sort of way. The preacher and other brethren certainly tried to reel her in but she didn't take the bait. There were too many "thou shall nots" to suit her. In the first place she figured a little nip now and then never hurt anybody. Angelina County stayed "dry," that is, liquor sales prohibited, until quite recently, but you could support your local bootlegger or take booze shopping trips to a neighboring "wet" county.

Aunt Mary didn't drink much but she did like a beer on a hot afternoon. She couldn't afford the bootlegger nor the "shopping trips" so she decided to keep a supply on hand by home brewing a batch every now and then. From a magazine she ordered a kit complete with a small vat, a bottle corker, and corks. The timing of the fermentation stage and bottling and corking was critical, but if all went according to Hoyle the beer tasted pretty fair. I know because, after I turned about 16 or 17, we'd both drink a cool one on the front porch. Except for a few folks she trusted, though, she kept quiet about her illegal and, according to some, sinful activity.

Once Aunt Mary miscalculated her timing and bottled a batch of "green beer" (that is, it hadn't finished fermenting). Lo and behold the preacher paid her a visit a few days later. A small room at the back of the house served as her "brewery," and as she and the preacher sat talking, there came a loud pop from that direction. She pretended to ignore it, then came another pop, then in a little while another one. The bottles were blowing their corks. Aunt Mary knew beer was spewing out all over the back room, but she went on with the conversation as nonchalantly as if the house was subject to pops at random intervals. If the preacher got wind of anything, so to speak, he didn't let on.

Aunt Mary never abstained from another "thou shall not," that is, talking raunchy. Back then, poking fun at anything between the navel and the knee caps was considered "vulgar" by the prim and proper and, by some, as sinful as cussing. This stopped almost no one, even some preachers and front row churchgoers who would never let a "vulgarity" cross their lips, from laughing at an off color crack.

Once the yard around the church Aunt Mary went to had grown into a thicket of elderberry bushes, and the church set aside a work day to clear them out. Aunt Mary ran into one of the church members in town along about then, and the woman said, "Mary, are you going to the church today? They're going to cut the elders." To which Aunt Mary replied, "If they're going to cut the elders, I don't see why they don't cut the deacons too."

Back when Aunt Mary was running the bus station café, a distant cousin of ours whom we called Aunt Flo lived right across the street in a big white painted house. She was by then an old woman and often went across to the café in the afternoon for a Coke or a cup of coffee. I seem to remember that Aunt Flo had been a chiropractor, but what I remember most is a characteristic that a lot of old people can sympathize with. A jet trail of sputtery farts often followed in her path.

One day some of us young'uns were "hanging out" at the café when Aunt Flo was there. When she emanated her "signature," we all started giggling, rather loudly I guess. Aunt Mary motioned for us to shut up. Now Aunt Mary would laugh at this too, but only after Aunt Flo had left. Aunt Mary also had a way of pretending she was fussing at young'uns when she was really just joshing around. After Aunt Flo had left that day, Aunt Mary started fussing at us this way, saying, "Now you young'uns ought to be ashamed of yourselves. Aunt Flo's an old woman and can't clinch 'em anymore."

Conversation didn't usually lag when Aunt Mary was around, but when it did she had some favorite expressions to un-lag it. Some were "clean" enough to say in front of the devout; others she self-censored. If family young'uns were around when things got quiet and still, she'd say,

"Hark, I thought I heard a pistol pop!" She'd pronounce the 'P's with a popping sound to make it clear that maybe somebody had farted. Amongst a select few grownups she'd say, "I want something so bad, but I don't know what. I guess I'll just go eat a banana."

Although Aunt Mary didn't give a hoot about the prevailing "thou shall nots" (she also smoked), she did have some strong religious beliefs. She mostly kept them to herself but every now and then she'd let one peek out. Once as just she and I stood around talking by the well, the subject of Jesus curing the woman at the well somehow came up. Aunt Mary said, "You know, we don't really understand how smart Jesus was. He taught in parables, and you have to be smart to do that. People could still talk in parables but they'd have to be mighty smart to know how." Then she changed the subject (and I will too).

A widow woman named Ella, called Miz Eller by everyone, lived across the road from Aunt Mary's and Uncle Kyle's house. She mangled the English language, and Aunt Mary often reported on her latest mangling. In some cases, Aunt Mary only had to repeat it verbatim; other times, I suspect, she exaggerated a little. Back then citrus fruit was a Christmas treat because it cost too much to have on a regular basis, so one Christmas somebody sent Miz Eller a box of tangerines.

Lots of country folks back then didn't bother with a Christmas tree, but they'd put out some kind of decoration or two. They'd hang up a stocking or a sprig of yaupon they'd plucked out in the woods. (Yaupon, a member of the holly family, bears red berries in the winter.) Aunt Mary preferred a fruit bowl in the center of the dining room table.

Folks visited back and forth a lot in those days and, one night just after Christmas, quite a bunch sat around Aunt Mary's dining table. She figured the fruit bowl had served its decoration purpose by then so she, and then the others, began munching on apples and pears and such. About that time, Miz Eller came over. After eyeballing the scene, she said: "Mary, if I'd a-knowed you 'as having a fruit supper, I'd have brung some ting-a-lings." Ever since then, in our family we refer to tangerines as "ting-a-lings."

20
Fiddling Around

Way back in the 1900s, a family in the settlement wanted to make sure their son wouldn't grow up to be a hardscrabble dirt farmer. Since the boy had some musical talent, they envisioned him someday playing in a big symphony orchestra in some big city. So they splurged and ordered him a "Strauss Concert Version" violin, which they informed everybody was a violin and not a fiddle. As has been known to happen a time or two in the past, the boy didn't share his parents' ambitions for him, and the violin was soon stuck back in a corner to gather dust.

Ever since the violin and fiddle evolved from the viol many hundreds of years ago, the instruments themselves have been essentially identical. They differ only in that the violin has traditionally been considered the aristocrat of the two and reserved for musicians who can read highbrow music. The fiddle, on the other hand, has long been relegated to the lower classes that play their jigs and reels (or Texas two-steps) by ear at taverns and at country dances. To demote the fiddle even lower, many folks used to swear that a frenzy of fiddling and dancing would call up the Devil.

Fast-forward a dab now to Dr. Rogers, our Uncle Merrill. By the time of this tale, he had retired his horse and buggy and invested in a Ford coupe for making house calls. In the little back jump seat, he kept his doctor's bag and pill supply ready for treating the sick, the infirm, the wounded, and the pregnant. He sometimes got paid a dollar or two, or maybe even five dollars for these visits, but mostly his patients paid him with eggs, a sack of sweet potatoes, a pretty good shovel, a quilt top, or whatever else they could rake up around the place that they figured he could use.

Along about in here, several members of the family with the non-violin playing son got sick in bed and sent for Uncle Merrill. After all of them had been doctored, the father brought out the dusty violin and, after explaining that it was a violin and not a fiddle, gave it to Uncle Merrill. So he thanked the man for the violin and put it in the coupe along with all his doctor paraphernalia.

Under the Black Gum Tree

On his way home, he stopped by at Grandpa's and Grandma's place, where they had just finished a round of hog killing. Grandpa noticed the violin right off and, when Uncle Merrill told him why it was stashed in the jump seat, Grandpa said, "I'll trade you two hams for that fiddle." To which Uncle Merrill replied, "I can use two hams a hell of a lot more than I can use that violin." And so the violin became a fiddle, and is still in the family.

Grandpa had always wanted some kind of musical instrument, and he told me that when he was a young teenager he even built himself a banjo. He said he cut a disk from a sturdy hardwood log, then whittled out the inside of the disk and smoothed it all out. He covered one side of the disk with a circular hunk of dried cowhide, then whittled out the neck, tuning pegs, etc. He tried stringing it with various things: thin strips of leather, dried pig gut, some strands of wire he found. He said he could sort of play it but that it didn't sound very good because he never could get a hold of the right kind of strings.

I never heard Grandpa play his violin-turned-fiddle, nor did hardly anyone else, but Mama told me he learned to play it tolerably well. She said that when he was feeling low he would take the fiddle out on the porch and play "Faded Love" (much, I suspect, as she would later peck out "Carry Me Back to Old Virginie" on the piano).

I learned a few years ago that he and Grandma once split the blanket. About all I know of the affair is that he left hearth and home to go live with another woman. I think I was in the first or second grade in Lufkin because Grandma came and stayed several days with us then. I recall that she was in tears when she arrived and shed many more before she left, and that the grownups treated her especially gently. Later, Grandpa sent word asking her to come home, and she took him back. In my later years I remember that they got along peaceably enough, but I never sensed much of a spark between them.

Grandma had a pump organ, but except for that and Grandpa's fiddle, very few folks in our neck of the woods owned a musical instrument. Those who could afford one (mostly males) favored the guitar, and the local churches managed to get a piano (often pronounced "pie-anner") long before they managed to paint the church house. Since nobody ever locked anything, the church piano was always available for anybody who wanted to go play it, including young'uns whose "Chopsticks" and plain old banging left most church pianos in an advanced state of decay. Nevertheless, several women became local legends because of their piano playing.

During the era of silent movies, Aunt Winnie played the background piano music at the picture show. Our neighbor Stella played, but she always claimed that her sister Florence was the better musician. The fancy fingering of either one of them, though, could turn even the sticking keys of an out-of-tune piano into a one-piece orchestra. Other women learned enough to at least play a one-finger melody with the right hand and throw in the usually correct chord with the left hand. Aunt Daisy (Grandpa's sister) could play a dab better than that, but since she was a Russell and roamed around in the woods a lot, red bug and tick bites interfered with her playing. That is, she couldn't play more than a few measures before she'd have to scratch. As Grandpa once put it, "Daisy could play all right if she'd quit scratching around under the piano bench."

These women and a few men played mostly by ear, although some could read "real music" and others played by shape notes. This method of musical notation dates back about a thousand years (really) so it's had a millennium, minus about the last 100 years, to be revised and tinkered with. It's based on the do-re-mi scale rather than the C, D, E, etc., of the standard, or "round note" method with all its scales and sharps and flats (that is, the black keys on a piano). The "tune" of the do, re, mi scale, as in the song "Doe, a deer, a female deer; ray, a drop of golden sun" and so on is the same for any standard scale (that is, key) from C, with no black keys, to the key of B, which uses them all.

The original purpose of shape-note music, way, way back yonder, was primarily as a means to teach "new" songs to singers, and in fact served that purpose over the centuries. Someone with a good ear for tones would first sing the song several times in its do, re, mi's, until everyone involved had memorized the tune. Then it could be sung with its words. By frontier times in the U.S., folks had begun applying this same method to playing whatever musical instrument they had available.

In shape note music, each do, re, mi tone is called a "syllable," so it's sort of to music what phonics is to plain old reading. Each syllable has its very own symbol: a square, a triangle pointed downward, a triangle pointed upward, and so forth. The names, number, and shapes of these syllables have differed considerably over the years. The original form, in about 1100 in Italy, used six syllables and threw in a combination of two of them to finish the seven-tone scale (that is, an octave). When the shape-note method got to England in about 1600, only four syllables were used with similar combinations required to round out the octave. The earliest

English colonists brought this form with them to North America where, by the early 1700s, it had become known as Sacred Harp music. For about the next 100 years, several seven-syllable schemes were devised. In the mid 1800s, all these got sent to shape note limbo in favor of Jesse Aiken's improved version.

In Aiken's method do, for instance, is always a triangle pointed upward for any octave and any key. In the key of C, this type triangle would be used for middle C, a low C way down in the bass, or a high C way up on the other end. Likewise, in the key of G, the upward pointed triangle would denote any G, or, in other words, the do tone in the key of G. Likewise, a half circle always denotes re, and so forth. All these shape notes are embedded in their proper place in the latticework of the lines and spaces of standard notation.

Reading shape-note music did require some knowledge of standard musical notation, but it relieved the player from having to figure out sharps and flats and from squinting to see in which line or space a plain old oval note was located. And, to some players, it served sort of like training wheels to reading "regular" music.

A professional musician recently told me that learning to read shape notes wasn't much easier than learning to read standard notation but, nevertheless, the method swept the country much as iPods have in our day. From about the mid 1800s until about World War II, printing presses turned out enough shape note music books, sheet music, and especially hymnals to reach from here to the Pearly Gates.

I still have a copy of Grandma's *Pentecostal Praise Hymnal*, copyright 1947, all printed in shape notes at 65 cents a copy. It includes a lot of the old familiar gospel songs, such as "I Come to the Garden Alone," "When the Saints Go Marching In," "Amazing Grace," and "The Old Rugged Cross." It also contains many more hymns that used to be familiar but aren't well known now, such as "Standing On the Promises," "Leaning On the Everlasting Arms," "This World is Not My Home," and one that is traditionally sung at funerals in our family, "When They Ring the Golden Bells." Another, "The Royal Telephone" (written in 1919), probably hasn't been sung for over 60 years, but was surely a sign of its time. Its first stanza:

> "Central's never busy, always on the line;
> You may hear from heaven almost any time;
> 'Tis a royal service, free for one and all,

When you get in trouble, give this royal line a call."

The scarcity of musical instruments never put a crimp in folks' hankering for music. They just went ahead and sang unaccompanied, even at dances. In the olden days, "play-party" games substituted just fine for square dancing, thank you very much. The dance steps were pretty much the same as those for square dancing, but followed the rhythm of vocalized tunes. Even folks who believed they would spend a hundred years in perdition for every single step they danced to a fiddle would high-step it in a play-party game. The standard repertoire of play-party tunes included:

> "Here we go loopti-lou,
> Here we go loopti-light
> Here we go loopti-lou,
> All on a Saturday night."

Or, probably more familiar:

> Verse 1: "Little red wagon painted blue,
>   (repeat twice)
> Skip to my lou, my lady"
> Chorus: Skip, skip, skip to my lou
>   (repeat twice)
> Skip to my lou my lady
> Verse 2: "Fly's in the buttermilk, shoo, shoo, shoo, etc.

Lots of folks, though, didn't need any special occasion to sing. Uncle Jack (Aunt Addie's husband and Grandpa's brother-in-law) often sang "Sally Goodin," and sang it loud enough that you could hear him from the house to the far end of the cornfield. Aunt Mary could usually come up with a song to fit any occasion. When I was a pre-teen, the movie *Springtime in the Rockies* came to the local picture show. For some reason we couldn't go to see it, but that didn't stop me from pestering the grownups to go anyway. I had just about worn out Mama's patience when Aunt Mary interrupted and sang the song "Springtime in the Rockies" all the way through. When she finished, she said to me, "Now see, you don't have to go now. Ever'thing that's in the show is in that song so you'd just be going through the same thing twice." That shut me up, but I didn't exactly believe her. (I still never have seen that movie.)

Sally Goodin

Had a piece of pie an' I had a piece of puddin',
An' I gave it all away just to see my Sally Goodin.
Well, I looked down the road an' I seen my Sally comin',
An' I thought to my soul that I'd kill myself a-runnin'.

Love a 'tater pie an' I love an apple puddin'
An' I love a little gal that they call Sally Goodin.
An' I dropped the 'tater pie an' I left the apple puddin'
But I went across the mountain to see my Sally Goodin.

Sally is my doozy an' Sally is my daisy,
When Sally says she hates me I think I'm goin' crazy.
Little dog'll bark an' the big dog'll bite you,
Little gal'll co'te you and' big gal'll fight you.

Rainin' an' a-pourin' an' the creek's runnin' muddy,
An' I'm so drunk, Lord, I can't stand studdy.
I'm goin' up the mountain an' marry little Sally,
Raise corn on the hillside an' the devil in the valley.

"Picking Up Paw-Paws," a favorite of Aunt Mary's and of the young'uns she taught it to, dates back to some pretty olden times, and might have been a play-party song. Native to the woods of eastern North America, the Paw-Paw tree (*Asimina triloba*) bears a small fruit that tastes like a banana. (Way up North, people call it the "Michigan Banana.") But through the years, the Paw-Paw tree fell into such obscurity that even its name got recycled and applied to the completely unrelated tropical Caribbean papaya. A move is now underway to grow the "original" Paw-Paw (or "Michigan Banana") commercially for its fruit.

"Picking Up Paw-Paws" is a happy song about pretty little Susie picking up the banana-tasting fruits and putting them into her pocket. It's full of "P" words, and Aunt Mary taught us to "pop" all these P's when we sang. That made the song even happier in our opinion because we improvised on our technique for "popping P's" until they resembled a vocal whoopee cushion.

The Paw-Paw Patch

Verse 1.	Where, O where is pretty little Susie?
	Where, O where is pretty little Susie?
	Where, O where is pretty little Susie?
	Way down yonder in the paw-paw patch.
Chorus:	Pickin' up paw-paws, puttin' um in her pockets,
	Pickin' up paw-paws, puttin' um in her pockets,
	Pickin' up paw-paws, puttin' um in her pockets,
	Way down yonder in the paw-paw patch.
Verse 2.	Come on, boys, let's go find her,
	Come on, boys, let's go find her,
	Come on, boys, let's go find her,
	Way down yonder in the paw-paw patch.

Not all our favorites were happy songs, though. I don't know why we humans are attracted to sad songs, but judging by their abundance we seem to need them. Our favorite one, "Babes in the Woods," should meet all but the most hardened soul's need for a sad song. It does contain an out-of-date reference that may affect the song's mental image but doesn't make it less sad. That is, its "strawberry leaves" probably did not come from strawberries as we know them.

The strawberry of shortcake fame does have a wild cousin that grows in the woods. It's a stringy plant that lies flat on the ground and bears berries not much bigger that an English pea. The equally miniature leaves from one plant would barely fill a teacup, and probably did not supply the leaves in the song. Rather, some unrelated strawberry-looking tree or bush seems a better candidate.

The early days of European settlers to North America must have been somewhat like those of Adam and Eve's in the Garden. In both cases they were surrounded by plants they didn't know the names of (Mark Twain once wrote that Eve went around Eden naming everything). The settlers sometimes kept the Indian names for plants, as I'd bet they did for the Paw-Paw, and certainly for the pecan, which Southerners have kept the Indian pronunciation for instead of "pee-can," as Northerners insist on calling it.

In other situations, the name for a "new" plant was based on its resemblance to a more familiar one (botanists sometimes do the same till this good day). At least one plant named this way had ample foliage for the "Babes in the Woods." Native from New York state south to Florida and east to Texas, the so-called strawberry bush (Euonymus americanus) grows to about eight feet tall and almost as wide. The reference in the song could have been to other strawberry look-alikes, but I nominate this one because it bears lots of squarish red fruit and, more indicative, has four-inch leaves.

Aunt Mary knew "Babes in the Woods" all the way through, and we used to beg her to sing it. She didn't always agree to sing it, but when she did, if we young'uns weren't in tears by the end of the second verse, we'd at least be mighty solemn.

I'm ending this chapter with the words to "Babes in the Woods" so you'll have time to dry your eyes before moving on to the next chapter.

Babes in the Woods

Verse 1:
My dear, don't you know
A long time ago
There were two little babes
Whose names I don't know
They were strollin' away
On a fair summer day
They were left in the woods
I've heard people say

Verse 2:
When it was night
So sad was their plight
The sun had gone down
And the moon gave no light
They sobbed and they sighed
And they bitterly cried
Then the poor little babes
They laid down and died

Verse 3: When they were dead
The little robins so red
Brought strawberry leaves
And over them spread
All the day long
They sang them this song
Poor babes in the woods
Poor babes in the woods
And don't you remember
The babes in the woods

21
Back at the House

By the late 1800s, the early settlers' cabins — some little more than shacks by today's standards — had been replaced by more permanent dwellings. These houses dotted the landscape for over a hundred years and, though still unplumbed and unpainted, they provided a goodly number of the comforts of home. But they were seldom called by that name.

When I was growing up, and no doubt long before, the word "home" was used sparingly. It was one of those words reserved for songs that could bring tears to your eyes, such as "My Old Kentucky Home," "Home on the Range," and "Home Sweet Home." Or else it was used to add emphasis in terms like "getting eaten out of house and home." Local newspapers sometimes used the word, especially when referring to the fancy painted houses in town, as in "The ladies met at the beautiful home of Doctor so-and-so."

But I don't remember that we ever invited anyone over to "our home." Instead we told them to "come over to the house." Likewise, we seldom had to "go home"; rather, we had to "get back to the house." We lived in "houses," and it would have been putting on airs to call them anything else. (Even till this good day, the sight of a "New Homes for Sale" sign in front of still raw housing developments raises my hackles.) Besides, as Grandma often pointed out, the Bible says our "real home is up yonder."

Grandpa's and Grandma's house, typical of many, many others, could have been plopped down in the middle of a present day East Texas pioneer village museum. It was square as a checkerboard with more doors than windows. A porch, which everyone called "the gal'ry" (gallery), ran the full length along the front.

From roughly March to October the gal'ry served for what would now be called both the living room and the family room (of which there was neither). There was a "porch" swing at one end that Grandpa had built, and a washstand with water bucket, dipper, and washbasin at the other end. In between were a bunch of straight- backed chairs and a rocking chair or two. The straight-backed chairs got carried back and forth from the gal'ry to wherever they were needed, often the dining room but also out to the wagon or the back of a pickup.

The seat of a wagon would only accommodate two adults or maybe three, depending on how stout they were. Young'uns sat on the floor of the wagon bed going to town, and on the sacks of flour and such on the way back. If there were more adults than the seat would hold, straight-backed chairs would be taken to the wagon for them to sit on. Later on, as pickups became more common, extra passengers would sit on chairs placed in the bed of the truck. When folks flagged down a passing pickup to catch a ride to town, they would take one of their own chairs from their gal'ry to sit on. I know first hand it was a bumpy ride, and to stay braced just right you had to sit high-rumped like you would on a skittish horse. But I never heard of anyone getting tossed over or out.

Some families preferred rawhide bottoms for their straight-backed chairs, and others liked cane bottoms. When cane bottoms had been sat upon long enough and often enough, they unraveled into a booby trap of spiky-splinters. I won't repeat any of the jokes that made the rounds about sitting on worn out cane-bottomed chairs. I'm sure you get the picture. Grandpa liked cane bottoms and made his own from the inner bark he stripped from hardwood logs. He would sit on the gal'ry and whittle and trim the strips to the right size and later soak and shape them. His knack for doing a good job at this was well known.

Franklin Roosevelt started all kinds of New Deal programs during the Depression. One of these guaranteed a free set of false teeth to anyone. Folks from all over were catching rides into Lufkin for their dental work. The high water mark of the process was "having your impression made." That is, after folks had endured having their teeth yanked out, they got to go in and sink their gums into a blob of putty. This would then form the mold for casting the dentures. So the main topic of most conversations was who all had their "impressions made" recently.

At about this time, a widow woman in the settlement sent word to Grandpa that her chairs needed re-caning. He sent word back to the woman that he would re-cane her chairs, but "she first had to come over and make her impression."

In our neck of the woods, at least, another New Deal program had everybody making mattresses. There was no market for cotton then, so farmers were given a set of lethal-looking mattress needles, free ticking, and told to pick and store their cotton. Grandpa and Grandma emptied the back room of the house and stored it there. Once a week folks took a load of their cotton down the road to the old dilapidated church house and made mattresses. These weren't meant to be sold, and everybody in the settlement ended up with enough mattresses to furnish a brothel. After the program ended, Grandpa stashed his set of mattress-making needles in their official-looking leather case on a ledge under the eaves of the gal'ry.

Besides sitting on the gal'ry, whittling on the gal'ry, washing up at the washstand and such, the gal'ry was where you sat to shell your black-eyed peas and butterbeans for dinner (at noon) or for canning. Any that fell on the floor, and a handful or so always did, got swept off into the yard for the chickens. All the pea hulls were collected in a bucket or basket and tossed to the cows. But you didn't let the cows have butterbean hulls because they have pointy ends that, it was said, would puncture the cows' innards.

The daily summertime ritual of shelling peas or beans wasn't limited to poor folks out in the country. Another Depression-era tale about more-well-off folks made the rounds. As the tale goes, a group of ladies in Lufkin who had never before needed to scrimp and save then had to gad around on a budget. They still had access to the family car, and gasoline was less than a dime a gallon. So every morning they would get together in groups of four or five and drive around sightseeing while they shelled their peas. That doesn't have much to do with the gal'ry, but its time to go into the house anyway.

From the gal'ry you could go to and from two places; the yard or the room sized hall. In the "dog trot" style of house, which numbered in the thousands in East Texas, the "hall" ran smack through the middle of the house. Wide open from the front to the back to let in any breeze that stirred, it was cooler than the rest of the house in the summer. Also, since it was under the house roof, it was dry in winter. It was thought to be warmer in winter than just being plain outside, and I guess it was because the dogs would "trot" into the hall and bed down on cold nights. I recall that what made the hall cooler in summer also made it drafty as an old barn in winter.

Many houses, such as Aunt Addie's and Uncle Jack's had this wide, open hall. Grandpa Bill's hall was open only at the front and ran about halfway back the depth of the house. Grandpa and Grandma walled theirs in on all four sides but put in extra wide doors at the front and back. They didn't use it for much, though, except to get from one part of the house to another.

Grandma put her fancy rosewood pump organ on one side of the hall. It looked fine but had been in bad musical shape for a long time, so nobody ever played it except us young'uns. Those of us who had the ability played tunes with various stops pulled out just to see how they'd sound: the rest just played around, pumping the pedals and making noise. Grandma later gave the organ to one of her preacher friends who, in turn, traded it for a thirty-five-dollar piano for his new church. Mama stayed riled up about this for years and said that, if she'd known what was going to happen, she'd have given the preacher thirty-five dollars.

Grandpa kept his two rifles, a .22 and a 25-caliber lever-action Marlin, and 12-gauge shotgun leaned up in a corner by the front door of the hall. They were always loaded and everybody, young'uns included, knew it and left them alone. In those days it was said a loaded gun was the safest since nobody except some damn fool, thinking it was empty, would mess around and have it go off and shoot somebody. Also, in those days grownups got mad even when a young'un pointed a toy gun at somebody else, and some young'uns got their butts whupped for doing that.

I never saw Grandpa shoot a gun but a few times. He used the Marlin rifle at hog-killing time but didn't encourage spectators for that. But I do know that he was an excellent marksman. Once a wild rooster nobody could get close to lived off scattered feed around the corncrib. One day Grandma got hungry for fried chicken and told me to take the .22 and go shoot it for dinner. After I shot several times at where the rooster had just been, Grandpa quietly took the rifle and dispatched the rooster on his first shot. (The fried chicken was kind of tough, but it tasted like a chicken should.)

There was often a double bed, probably outfitted with mattresses made at the old church house, on one side of the hall for cooler sleeping in the summer, and for colder sleeping (usually by young'uns or youngish company) in winter. But the only other major use of the hall was for the telephone. It was the old-timey party-line, crank type mounted on the wall in the same corner where Grandpa kept his guns.

Alexander Graham Bell invented the telephone in 1876 and, in only a few years, phones became more or less commonplace in major cities all over the world. By the early 1900s, phone service was available in rural areas of the U.S. and, in fact, folks who lived out in the "sticks" could have phones long before they got electricity (about 35 years later in our neck of the woods).

The telephone "instrument" itself was, and still is, a marvel of engineering design with its hand-crank-driven magneto for the ringer and its battery-powered diaphragms in the earpiece and mouthpiece. But the area-wide distribution wiring was just slightly less primitive than a bunch of tin cans hooked up together with string. The best thing you could say about it is that it worked some of the time.

A single wire was strung from the telephone office in Huntington out into a settlement and fastened to some handy support — a tree, a fence post, maybe some few and far between "homemade" telephone poles. If the line got knocked down by the wind or by a roaming cow, nobody on that line had phone service until somebody went out and refastened the line.

From this line, single wires were tapped off and run into the houses of those who could afford phone service. There was no ground wire; you had to supply your own. A metal rod was driven into the ground at someplace that stayed damp, often near the well, and the ground "wahr" (that is, wire) run from there to the phone. When phone conversations got staticky or weak, the standard routine was to tell someone, usually a young'un, to "go pour a dipper of water over the ground wahr!"

Conversations were never private. A sort of code or "PIN" based on the number and type of "rings" assigned to each household identified the calls intended for that phone (Grandma's and Grandpa's was two short rings) and every "PIN" rang on every phone on that party line. People all up and down the line chimed in, no matter who the call was for, and not secretively either. They announced who they were and got in on the conversation. But most calls were short and to the point; idle chitchat was rare. Some teenagers did figure out early on that they could play pranks over the phone but usually whomever they called caught on right off the bat.

One time, though, when Uncle Dale was in his late teens, he disguised his voice and called Aunt Daisy. He told her he was from the phone company and they were fixing a problem. He said they had to blow out the lines and that she should put a paper bag over her phone or else all the dust would blow out into her house. He swears that she believed him and did as she was told.

Most Piney Woods houses had only one fireplace in, of course, the "fireplace room," usually located next to the hall. Much of the "living" that took place on the gal'ry in summer was moved into this "fireplace room" in winter. It wasn't exactly what we'd call a living room, even though it was where everyone sat, whether family or company, day or night. There was a double bed in it for the husband and wife of the household, usually a chifforobe, rocking chairs brought in from the gal'ry, and straight-backed chairs as needed. A table somewhere in the room accommodated all sorts of things: a coal-oil lamp, a clock, recent mail, maybe some photographs, and, after about the mid-1930s, a radio.

The fireplace and chimney (often pronounced "chimlee") were homemade using few store-bought materials. Wattle and daub is the official name of the construction technique used but most people back then didn't know, or care, what it was called. They first built a framework out of stout posts then latticed it with a bunch of wooden slats. They then brought in a load of clay or sticky mud from some creek bed and plastered or "stuccoed" it on the lattice inside and out. These chimneys should have been re-plastered every few years, but many weren't and the slats showed through where the "plaster" had eroded away. Bricks or cement were usually store-bought for the fireplace and hearth, although rocks or any other kind of fireproof material that could be rounded up were sometimes used.

As is well known, these fireplaces could blister you on one side while leaving your other side frosty. One way to even out the temperature a dab on your back and front was (and is) to frequently replace the "back stick" (called the backlog in other parts). Keeping a good-sized chunk of unburned wood at the back of the fireplace and the "burning wood" in front of it creates a draft that throws the heat outward into the room instead of up the chimney. The back stick flames up slower than the other wood, and when it does and starts burning down, it's pulled forward and replaced. In the olden days, a common saying when the room started chilling down was "put another back stick on the fahr."

Back in those days, when folks came in from outside in the winter, they'd throw their coats, and sometimes their hats, on the bed and go stand by the fire to warm up. A superstition held that putting a hat on a bed brought bad luck, so some folks put their hats somewhere else. But plenty of other people didn't hold with that. There were also plenty of folks who chewed tobacco or dipped snuff, so when they came in they'd make a beeline to go spit in the fireplace. There's an old tale about the man who came into a fireplace room where a pretty girl was sitting. When he saw her, he got so flustered he threw his hat in the fire and spit on the bed!

Old-timey wind-up phonographs became available several years before radios did. A few people bought them, including Grandpa Bill, but nobody had many records. Aunt Mary said Grandpa Bill had only one, a comedy routine by two men talking to one another. One's name was Jiggs, but Aunt Mary couldn't remember the other's name. She said that the record wasn't funny, but they sat around in his fireplace room many a winter night listening to it over and over again.

The radio remedied this kind of monotony, that is, when the battery was charged (remember that there was no electricity). These early radios didn't have nice little internal batteries like we're used to now. Most people got a car battery and placed it on the floor under the radio. It stayed charged up long enough to run for a few weeks. When the battery ran down, it had to be carried to the garage in town to be recharged. Since people didn't go to town very often, it could be weeks before it got recharged. During this period, folks again "did like they do across the river," that is, they did without. But when it was working, people followed what became a ritual.

We turned the radio on for the local news at noon to find out who all had died, who all were on the sick list, who had company from "way off," and so on. Enough air time was usually left after this for a live performance by a local singer, choir, or piano player. Young'uns who wanted to do something special (or, whose parents wanted them to) were always accommodated. One of my cousins remembers that, when she was a very little girl, her grandmother (Grandma Wade) took her to the radio station to recite a verse.

After the news, we listened to the Light Crust Doughboys, a men's ensemble sponsored by the Light Crust Company in Fort Worth. They sang and played foot-tapping renditions of everything from old dance tunes to hymns. When their program ended, it was time for a nap, then back to work.

Our favorites, though, were on Saturday night. The programs started about the same time people in the southern U.S. finished supper, and went on till nearly midnight. I don't recall all of them; one was the *Louisiana Hayride* out of Shreveport. Then there was some kind of barn-dance program and *then* —everybody's favorite — *The Grand Ole Op'ry*! We listened to Roy Acuff and Minnie Pearl and Grandpa Jones and Chet Atkins and Little Jimmie Dickens and over a dozen others.

They sang and played what was then called "hillbilly music," which uppity people in towns and cities looked down on and mostly couldn't abide. In fact, in some circles, if people found out you liked hillbilly music, or worse, if you played it, you'd be relegated to ignoramus status before you could strum a single chord.

To my way of thinking, something got lost in the progression from hillbilly music to today's style of Country–Western. With all its amplifiers and sequined costumes and bright red cowboy boots and fireworks, it just doesn't have that "down-home" feeling. *The Grand Ole Op'ry* performers struck a chord (no pun intended, or maybe it was) with people out in the sticks like us. They were like homefolks or kinfolks who just happened to live a ways off so we hadn't had a chance to meet them yet.

They'd have been right at home in our house. They could have walked into the fireplace room, put their guitar cases on the double bed, pulled up some straight-backed chairs and started pickin' and singin' songs like "The Wabash Cannonball" and "The Great Speckled Bird." And we'd have gone through many a back stick carrying on and listening to them.

A front room and a back room were usually located on the other side of the hall. Our tour of these two rooms won't take long because not much noteworthy ever happened in them. Company and young'uns —and, from time to time, a boarder — slept in them, so I guess we'd call them bedrooms (the front room had two double beds and the back room one). The front room was really more an all-purpose room where Grandma kept her old treadle Singer and did her sewing. The back room was a catchall room where you might find anything.

During some winters one of the small, flimsy-sheet-metal wood stoves that didn't last as many seasons as it cost in dollars, would be set up in the front room, especially if there was a paying boarder. The back room was not heated, and thus was avoided in winter except for dashing in to grab something. A homemade rack of shelves took up one of its walls. By the end of the summer, the shelves were loaded with canned goods, and by the next spring with empty canning jars.

There were trunks in both rooms since, back then, that's where folks kept their linens, quilts, everyday clothes, and such. Because they didn't have an oversupply of any of these, two or, at most three, trunks per family were enough. A trunk tale that I recall is about a family that had a big, strapping grownup "boy" still living at home.

In the Piney Woods, banana pudding made with real bananas, custard, and vanilla wafers was (and still is) considered ambrosia from the gods. Besides tasting "divine," as someone once said, it was a special treat because you only had these ingredients when you'd just been to town. As the story goes, this "boy's" mama had gotten all this and made a great big banana pudding while her son was at work.

The family knew if he found it when he got home, he'd eat the whole thing before anybody even sat down for supper. They pondered over where to hide it and decided on putting it in the trunk in the back room. After supper, when the boy's mama went to get the pudding out of the trunk for dessert, all she found was an empty bowl!

Watermelons also ranked way up there on the favorite list. In the summer all the households in the settlement had a watermelon patch and kept several handy for slicing. We'd sometimes go pick two or three, then eat them straight out of the field. Their temperature ranged from warm to very warm, and they tasted fine, but a cooler melon hit the spot better. If you've ever wondered why cats catnap under a bed in the summer, it's because it's cooler there; maybe the mattress acts as an insulator. And that's where we kept a supply of watermelons: under the bed in the back room.

I've said earlier that, during the mattress-making episode, Grandma and Grandpa stored their cotton in the back room. Another time they stored their peanut crop there, to let it cure and dry, I suppose. The crop was for livestock feed, so the room was stuffed to nearly the ceiling with entire peanut plants. I remember that the room smelled just like the haystack it had become, and that it was the perfect place for young'uns to play. As I look back, I wonder how many people have childhood memories of sliding around on a real haystack in the bedroom and gobbling up raw goobers all the while.

Typical Piney Woods Farmhouse of the type that replaced the rustic cabins, circa 1900s

22

GRANDMA WADE'S FOURTH HUSBAND

Recall that Grandma Wade's first husband, Pat Sowell, died while she was pregnant with their third child (Cora). Several years later she married J. C. Simmons who wasn't good to her and she left him. She then stayed husbandless until she married A. J. Wade, who died seven years later. She stayed husbandless on this go around for the next 23 years.

At just a few years shy of 80, she got a hankering to try her luck at marriage once again. I don't know which came first, the hankering or Old Man Snaveley (not his real name), but I suspect the former because Old Man Snaveley sure wasn't much to stir up a hankering. At any rate, she married him along about 1940 and they lived a little ways out from "downtown" Huntington.

I spent a few days with them several times when I was in elementary school. Their place sat on an acre or so of a knoll overlooking a patch of pines across the road. A stand of "real" woods bordered the back of the property. Their house — an old, sort of fixed-up farmhouse — had a big front and side porch, but no indoor plumbing or electricity. They did have a telephone and a radio. Two things stand out in my mind about these visits.

Grandma Wade always laid in a supply of light bread, peanut butter and bananas before I got there. Several times a day she'd fix me a sandwich by smushing up some bananas and peanut butter together then spreading it on light bread. (That's the way a peanut butter and banana sandwich should be fixed, that is, not messed up with mayonnaise or big slices of banana.) And I got to eat as many of these sandwiches as my little heart desired.

The other thing I remember is that I steered clear of Old Man Snaveley, which wasn't easy since he always sat around somewhere on the porch or in the house. He was grumpy, gruff, and just generally unpleasant. Grownups also avoided him. I several times overheard them refer to him as a "mean old man," but it didn't stop them from visiting Grandma Wade.

In one case a young husband and his pregnant wife went by to visit, and the husband warned the wife ahead of time not to even look at Old Man Snaveley lest he put the "evil eye" on her and botch the pregnancy.

Uncle John, Grandma Wade's son, always seemed to need a job, a place to stay, or both. He'd try to live with his own family from time to time, but he and his wife didn't get along so he'd pretty soon either leave or she'd throw him out. At some point he worked as a seaman on merchant ships out of Galveston, which solved both the job and the living quarters problem for a while. For another period he traveled around with a carnival.

He ran one of those baseball pitch stalls with a lot of Teddy bears, plaster figurines, knickknacks, and a few "super prizes" on display. You could win one of these if you aimed and pitched hard enough to knock down a vertical, pyramid shaped stack of "dolls." We called them "dolls," which they did look like, but they were actually sort of disguised bowling pins weighted so much at the bottom that they wouldn't topple no matter how sizzling the pitch.

Uncle John quit this endeavor sometime in the late 1930s and stayed with Grandma and Grandpa for a while. He stashed the "dolls" and baseballs in their smoke house and there they remained for many years except when we young'uns took them out to play with. We threw all kinds of things, including chunks of old rusty iron, at the dolls without, as I recall, ever getting them to do more than keel over a little bit. We even tried to shoot them down with our B-B guns and slingshots, but that was wishful thinking.

Uncle John tried his hand at another thing or two after this, then moved in with Grandma Wade and Old Man Snaveley. I don't know how the three got along during the several months they lived together but, judging by the way it ended, there must have been stormy times.

One summer Sunday afternoon, Uncle John and Old Man Snaveley disagreed over what radio program to listen to. The argument heated up until Old Man Snaveley's temper flared. Uncle John then went out and sat down on the gal'ry. Old Man Snaveley went and got his gun and proceeded to shoot Uncle John at close range. One shot was all it took. Old Man Snaveley, gun in hand, then went running off into the woods behind the house.

Grandma Wade called the Sheriff, who put together a posse right quick. They fanned out and began searching the woods. They knew they were on the right track and getting closer to Old Man Snaveley. Then, from a little ways ahead, they heard one shot. Old Man Snaveley had turned the gun on himself.

The news got around as it does in a small town, but neither the paper nor the radio publicized it much. Grandma Wade lived out her remaining 11 years, once again husbandless.

Uncle John is buried in the family cemetery. Nobody knows, or cares, who claimed Snaveley's body or where it is buried. He was clearly a troubled man, we'll never know over what. Nor will we know why Grandma Wade thought it worth her time to marry him.

#8 UNDER THE BLACK GUM
UNCLE JOSH IN THE CORRAL

Once upon a time railroad tracks connected little country towns in the Piney Woods with the rest of the country. Trains stopped to load cotton bales from local gins and live cattle that farmers had herded to the railroad corral, and to unload grocery staples and such. From the early 1900s until after World War II they made regular stops at Huntington's now long gone depot, where Uncle Josh (husband of Aunt Minnie, Grandpa's sister) was stationmaster. Josh and Minnie lived and raised their family in the railroad's mustard yellow painted house right across a lane from the depot.

Thanks to Aunt Minnie, tales about Uncle Josh periodically circulated. Back after vitamins had been discovered and their benefits praised, Uncle Josh jumped on the band wagon and bought a packet. Along about that time Aunt Minnie got ahold of some special bean seeds and put them in an envelope on top of the icebox to save until spring. At planting time she found nary a bean seed in the envelope. Uncle Josh had swallowed one a day and told everyone how much better he felt.

Similarly, in his later years he complained of getting deaf (pronounced "deef") and bought a hearing aid. He wore it religiously and told one and all he could hear better than he ever had. Later, when one of his grown sons stopped by for a visit, he asked Uncle Josh how long the battery lasted. Uncle Josh answered that he'd never had to replace it. At that, the son took the hearing aid and opened the battery compartment. It contained nary a sign of a battery.

Uncle Josh took his railway job seriously and guarded the premises like a bulldog. One dark and windy night he spied a figure dressed all in white next to the railroad corral, which was full of cattle waiting to be shipped. He told Aunt Minnie that somebody was trying to steal some cows, then grabbed his shotgun and slipped over into the corral. He couldn't make out the figure very good in the dark, but its arms and legs seemed to be flailing around. So he crouched down behind the cattle's water trough and got ready to shoot in case things got dicey.

Back in the olden days, banana bunches for shipment were wrapped snuggly in heavy paper cut and stapled into a cone shape. The grocery store next door to the depot had recently received such a bunch, and the grocer had thrown the paper cone out the back door onto his trash pile.

Just after Uncle Josh crouched down, the wind picked up the cone and blew it smack dab over the head of one of the cows. All hell broke loose in the corral. Cows ran around in a bellowing and shitting confined stampede. Several jumped over the water trough, knocking Uncle Josh into it. During the commotion, Uncle Josh accidentally pulled the trigger.

When things simmered down he eased over to check out the would-be cattle thief. He was pretty sure he'd hit it, but its arms and legs still flailed around, as they should have on a windy night. Aunt Minnie had washed his long-handled underwear that day and left it hanging on a line by the corral. He had shot his own union suit!

OLD HUNTINGTON GAS STATION

23
THE DIPPING VAT

Till this good day my brothers and I call blue denim overalls "Uncle Jack overalls" because that's what he always wore. And I'm reminded of Aunt Addie when I hear the word "snuff" even though today it does not always refer to powdered tobacco. Both lived a long time, she for 91 years, and he for 89. They often teased one another, and let the other do as he or she pleased, no matter how wacky, without getting riled up or passing judgment. They died within a few months of each other in 1968.

When any of us young'uns went to see them, as we often did, Aunt Addie would sit down and between dips and spits of snuff talk to us like we had some sense. When Uncle Jack came in from whatever he'd been doing, he'd tweak our noses and make some kind of silly sound like we didn't.

One of the many back roads, not much more than lanes, that led off through stretches of woods to other farms separated Aunt Addie's and Uncle Jack's farm from Grandma's and Grandpa's. I walked to their place sometimes and other times rode my horse Nellie. On these visits Aunt Addie told me tales about the olden days and our family history, which I have sprinkled throughout these pages. She also told me about plucking geese.

Old-timey bedsteads (pronounced "bedstids") consisted of head and foot "boards" often made of iron, onto which metal side rails attached. Wooden bed slats rested on the side rails. Bedsprings of the open metal springs variety sat on top of the slats. Then came the mattress. Before air conditioning and central heating folks slept on cotton mattresses in summer and feather ones in winter.

Aunt Addie said plucking geese was about as hard and dirty a job as had to be done. In the first place you have to pluck many a goose to get a mattress's worth of feathers, and geese are mean and remarkably strong. You have to clamp the flapping and snapping goose under one armpit with the hind end of its belly pointed upward in your lap. Then while it squawks and strains you pluck the soft down on its belly with your other hand right quick before the goose gets loose. And geese are not potty trained. After you and the down have been cleaned, you can stuff the mattress ticking.

We all saw and often killed, as was the practice back then, snakes of various kinds. But we almost never saw a rattler even though we knew they slithered around in the woods. They usually stayed out of sight, maybe because of their natural camouflage. (Once, from my truck, I saw a big diamondback in the middle of a lane and watched as it slithered over to an oak and wrapped itself around the base of a tree. Its coloration matched the bark so well that I could not see it anymore, even though I knew it was there.) Aunt Addie said they did see one in the yard one day but it darted off before they could kill it.

Not long after that Aunt Addie and Uncle Jack heard a sort of rustle under the bed in the middle of the night, but didn't pay any attention to it. It happened again the next night, and on the third night rustled enough to tweak a bedspring. When it got daylight, they looked under the bed but didn't see anything but floor. So they took the mattress and covers out in the yard, thinking maybe a mouse had moved in. It all looked okay. Then they checked the bedsprings and, sure enough, a rattlesnake had camouflaged its coils inside the coils of one of the bedsprings.

When I visited at Aunt Addie's and Uncle Jack's I always liked to check out the dipping vat. Back during the Depression, the Federal government set up many programs to improve the lot of farm folks across the country. These included developing new ways to raise healthier livestock. From before Methuselah till now cattle have been plagued by all sorts of flies and biting insects. The resulting itching and blood loss, and often infection and disease, takes its toll on livestock health. I don't know what they did in Methuselah's day, but I bet they smeared some kind of deterrent on their cattle and camels. (Maybe Noah did too as he loaded the Ark.)

Anyway, in one form or another, a smearing approach was long used all over the world. In the olden days folks dipped a tow sack (that is, a burlap bag) into a tubful of some kind of oil and then wiped a cow or horse with it. They often put the smearing off till another day, though, and often did a half-assed job (yes, that part of the anatomy gets bug bit too). During the Depression, to improve the situation, the government built dipping vats here and there throughout farming and ranching country. Instead of smearing animals, the dipping vat soaks them. And the one for our neck of the woods was built on Aunt Addie's and Uncle Jack's place.

Built of concrete, it looked like a swimming pool except that it was only a little wider than the girth of a fat cow or huskier bull. Rainwater kept it full. Cattle walked into the vat, one at a time, via a ramp at its front end. Then the vat deepened to about five feet so they had to swim to another ramp at the other end. Sturdy corrals with narrow cattle chutes were built at each end of the vat so a cow could get out of one corral and into the other only by taking a swim. Periodically some kind of oily "bug" repellent or, maybe, insecticide was poured into it. I don't know what this substance was, only that it smelled somewhat like creosote, and a brownish oily sheen always covered the water surface.

Seldom used, the dipping vat was abandoned within a few years. Local farmers, several of whom didn't cotton to new ideas anyway, found it a hassle to drive their cows back and forth to be dipped. By the time I always liked to check it out, scummy algae had joined the oily sheen on the water surface. But I always thought that one day the water would clear up and I could go for a swim.

Uncle Jack did cotton to some of the new Depression era ideas, and, as did many other farmers, he especially admired Henry Wallace.

Born into a well off and influential Iowa family, Wallace began his strange career as editor of Wallace's Farmer, a journal founded by his grandfather to popularize the benefits of scientific agriculture. Although a Republican, Wallace served as Secretary of Agriculture during President Franklin Roosevelt's first two terms and, in 1940, Wallace was elected F.D.R.'s Vice President.

His career then started downhill. He feuded with people he should have kowtowed to, and vice versa. At one point he trusted a con man and although he finally saw the light and broke off with him, it damaged Wallace's reputation, especially in Washington. He more and more became a believer in mystic religions. When the 1944 election rolled around, F.D.R. dumped him in favor of Harry Truman for V.P. After F.D.R.'s death, when Truman became President and the Cold War had set in, Wallace spoke out against the "get tough on Russia" movement. This really ruined his rep with the mainstream but won him support among Communists, of which he seemed completely oblivious. In 1948 Wallace ran for President as a Progressive. He came in fourth behind Truman, Dewey, and Strom Thurmond (a Dixiecrat). Wallace then retired to his experimental farm in upstate New York and died in 1965 of Lou Gehrig's disease.

Henry Wallace is generally remembered now, if at all, as an activist for socialism. But in his day, despite his blunders in electoral politics, several higher-ups declared that he was the best Secretary of Agriculture the country ever had. And, today, historians taking a look back agree that the "new" scientific farming methods he pioneered have now become standard practice. Wallace worked hard to develop hybrid seed that yielded better crops. He led the development of soil conservation techniques to prevent erosion. He took steps to improve animal health and prevent livestock disease.

Uncle Jack might have been a Wallace devotee because of socialistic views. Mama once told me confidentially that Uncle Jack had socialistic notions and was a big fan of Henry Wallace. Or Uncle Jack could have become a believer in the new ways. He did, after all, set aside the land for the dipping vat. And although the "new ways" mostly took hold and helped big farmers elsewhere, some of them made it into the Piney Woods.

Grandpa's favorite corn variety, "Hastings Prolific," was a hybrid. And although folks poked fun at Ag Agents, they did some good work. In a water conservation and erosion control project, they helped local farmers contour and terrace their fields. Grandpa's field had a slight but definite slope, so they spaced and laid out wider and higher contour rows between the regular rows to control rainwater run off. Grandpa's field didn't need but a few contour rows, and he always grew watermelons on them.

Once when an outbreak of Black Leg among East Texas cattle seemed likely, the Government supplied communities including ours with vaccine. This aptly named disease is spread by a highly virulent soil borne bacteria (Clostridium Chauvdei) that can deposit its reproductive spores on blades of grass and other low-growing plants. If a cow grazes on this, the spores get into its blood stream through punctures (even little bitty ones) in the intestinal lining. The spores then divide and re-divide into more and more bacteria. This leads to toxemia (that is, blood poisoning) because the cow's innards can't handle the bacterial overload. Black Leg can be fatal in as few as 12 to 14 hours.

I remember vaccination day. So many youngish folks had moved off to various lands of regular paychecks that the job fell to several elderly men helped out by one teenaged girl. A deserted farmstead down the road a piece still had a sizable corral in good shape, and over 20 head of the free ranging cattle (including one bad bull) had been penned up in it.

The first order of business that day was to chat, so the men pushed their hats to the back of their heads to show they were in no hurry. After a while each readjusted his hat firmly down across his forehead and got to work. Things mostly went quietly and smoothly. While one man filled the syringe, others cornered an animal and got a rope around its neck. No rodeo antics, no lassoing, no wrestling an animal to the ground and hogtying it. A man just eased up and slipped a noose over the animal's head. While the "rope man" kept the animal still, the "syringe man" eased over and jabbed it in the hindquarter.

My job was to keep the men supplied with ropes, open the gate and help drive a vaccinated animal out of the corral, and run fetch things. I did get to be the "rope person" for a few docile calves. One of these danced sideways just as the "syringe man" took aim and almost jabbed me instead of the calf. I used to think that if he had jabbed me I'd be immune to Black Leg, but I later learned that the bacteria don't take up residence in human innards.

We did have one rodeo whoop-te-do. It took just about all the ropes, lots of "run fetches," and a good half hour of close encounters to subdue the big bad bull. After the men had attached ropes to almost all of his extremities, the "syringe man" dashed in, jabbed, and dashed back. The rodeo continued as all the ropes were unattached, after which we yanked open the gate and the bull snorted out. We then all pushed our hats to the back of heads.

Nothing remains of that old deserted farmstead. For many years a few of the original jonquils sprouted and bloomed in the spring, but they too finally gave up the ghost. In fact, such "old-house places" as they are called, can sometimes be identified by patches of jonquils and maybe some scraggly rose bushes.

A couple of years before Aunt Addie and Uncle Jack died, they left their farm and moved to a sort of "modern house" close to town. Their "new" yard had been neglected, so Aunt Addie pretty quick planted lots of flowers and shrubs, including a lilac. She couldn't coax it to bloom, though, so she decorated it Christmas-tree style with pictures of lilac blossoms she'd cut out of garden catalogues.

Uncle Jack's and Aunt Addie's "old" farmhouse is now also long gone. The property still belongs to the family and has been used as pasture land for a good while. But though crumbling in some places and overgrown with brush, the dipping vat is still there. If in the distant future archeologists discover its ruins, I bet they'd never figure out that it was used to debug cattle.

A young Uncle Jack hauling logs out of the woods, circa early 1900s

24
UNCLE THEDFORD

Somebody once said Uncle Thedford (Grandpa's brother) had female trouble. At any rate he had a wife and couldn't keep her, then another likewise. (I guess he didn't try the pumpkin shell approach.) Except maybe for his two exes, he was everyone's buddy, though. Even with the difference in our ages he certainly rated as one of my buddies, partly because he stayed boyish throughout his 77 years.

His first wife, Bobbie, up and left him one day while he was at work. That would have been in the early 1900s, and she loaded everything in the house into the wagon and took off. As Uncle Thedford was going back home that day he found a pillow in the middle of the road. He began to get the picture a little while later when he found and recognized a churn also in the middle of the road. They had fallen off the wagon and, in her haste to get away, Bobbie didn't stop to retrieve them. So Uncle Thedford got home to an empty house. They had no children, and he always said he only got a pillow and a churn out of that marriage.

Although Johnnie Clyde, Uncle Thedford's second wife, left him in a less dramatic way than Bobbie had, she did leave him with two sons. And that ended his female troubles as far as we know.

Uncle Thedford worked at one thing and another all his life but never had much in his wallet to show for it. This began early since his Daddy (Grandpa Bill) always worked his boys hard. Once Grandpa Bill put a young Thedford and his older brother Jimmy to work digging a well.

In those low-tech days, they needed only a shovel and a couple of buckets. While one of them dug up a bucket of dirt the other took the filled bucket off a ways and dumped it. After several days the hole was deeper than the "boys" were tall, so they rigged up a rope and pulley for getting in and out of the hole and for hoisting up the filled bucket.

At this time the family had an old blind cow that they kept a bell on so they'd always know if she was wandering off into harm's way. One day when Uncle Thedford was working topside, he yelled down to Uncle

Jimmy that he'd go get them a drink of water. Instead he went and got the bell from the cow.

Then, jingling the bell the way the cow did, he slipped back to the hole. He hunched down, still jingling the bell, and pushed a chunk or two of surface dirt down into the hole. After only a few chunks had rained down, Uncle Jimmy began hollering, "Thedford! Thedford! Hurry up and get back here! That old cow's about to fall right on top of me!"

Uncle Thedford didn't mind working, but he was cut out for a non-energetic job that allowed him to mix work with play and to socialize with everyone. He found this niche in his late middle age. He served several terms as Constable in Huntington, which needed a Constable about like a hog needs a hairdresser. I suspect folks voted for him because the job paid enough for him to get by on and gave him something to do.

He might have broken up a fistfight or witnessed the signing of some official paper from time to time. But his duties, as he saw them, were about the same as those of the "Greeter" at Wal-Mart. He could blow the whistle on the equivalent of a shoplifter, but the Sheriff handled the few messy things that came up, such as arresting somebody. So Uncle Thedford just strolled around town chatting with folks and spreading cheer.

He often ate at Aunt Mary's café. He didn't expect a free lunch, but he figured out an unusual way to pare down his meal expenses. He'd buy a pork chop at the grocery store then ask her to cook it for him. Aunt Mary, of course, would never have set a big plate containing only a lonesome pork chop in front of him, so she loaded it up with the veggies on the menu that day. Since her profit margin was thin as cellophane and about as invisible, she once confided that it would help if every now and then he'd pay her the price of a vegetable plate.

After Uncle Thedford retired from the constabulary he lived with one sibling for a while and then another. He earned his keep by helping with the farm work and they all tolerated one another pretty well, but for one reason or another he'd eventually move on.

Once, when he was living with Aunt Addie and Uncle Jack, a crony in town asked him if Addie treated him all right. He hesitantly answered, "Yeah, I guess so," to which the man asked, "What's the matter? Don't she feed you good?" Uncle Thedford answered, "Oh yeah, she feeds me real good." So the man said, "Well then, do you have a good bed to sleep in?" Uncle Thedford replied, "Well, that's the problem." So the man asked several more questions: "Is the mattress lumpy?" "No" "Do you have warm quilts?" "Yes." The man finally asked, "Then what's the matter with your bed?" The answer: "Well, Addie don't turn down the covers for me at night."

I was in my teens when Uncle Thedford moved in with Grandma and Grandpa. He helped with the plowing and I with various chores but we still had time to buddy around together. We sometimes went squirrel hunting, although we never shot one or for the matter even saw one, probably because we chattered so much we scared them all off.

Grandma often sent us to the garden to pick a bucket or two of vegetables for dinner. We always picked some extra tomatoes and cucumbers just for the two of us right then and there. We'd go sit in the shade under a tree, and Uncle Thedford would brush the dirt off of them with his shirt tail then slice them up with his (probably filthy) pocketknife. We snacked on those sun-warmed slurpy tomatoes and cool, thin cucumber slices until we figured we'd better take Grandma her supply for the table.

Folks here and there still have Martin boxes, and back in the olden days most farmsteads had at least one. Martins, small birds in the swallow family, gulp down scores of flying insects each day. The males are an iridescent, almost blackish, purple and the females a drabbish brown with a splash of white. Big flocks of them nest cheek by jowl. Martin boxes, a sort of avian condominium, have from six to over a dozen individual pigeon-hole-sized birdhouses under the same roof. Back then, before sprays and rub on repellants, a thriving colony of Martins devoured enough mosquitoes to make sitting on the porch a pleasure instead of a swatting, scratching frenzy. Grandpa always built his own Martin box, usually with 12 "apartments," and mounted it atop a tall, stout pole in the front yard.

We all, including Uncle Thedford and me, always watched the Martins while we rested on the front porch during the heat of the afternoon. They flew around swooping up insects and came back to the box just long enough to feed their little ones. Then one day they started hovering around their nests and squawking like a flock of crows. We all noticed this change but from our vantage point on the ground didn't see anything wrong. After a few days we saw the problem. A fair-sized chicken snake stuck its head out of one of the holes.

Grandpa carefully unfastened the pole and lowered the whole shebang. When the snake poked its head out enough he grabbed it by the neck and dispatched it to its just reward. While he remounted the Martin box, Uncle Thedford and I took the snake carcass off a good ways from the house to examine it. Uncle Thedford slit its belly open with his pocketknife. It contained a wad of birds, we couldn't tell exactly how many, but that snake had been well fed. The Martins, no doubt rejoicing in bird fashion, returned to their normal routine.

Uncle Thedford lived for several more years after this, hale and hearty until his last days. Except for maybe his pocketknife he left no mementoes folks could point to and say, "That belonged to Thedford." Likewise, he left slim pickings for the conventional type of obituary that paints the deceased as a perfect model of virtue and gumption.

He loved to play dominoes with his cronies but some folks, Grandma especially, firmly believed that the road to Hell is paved with as many dominoes as good intentions. He left no civic legacy, such as Grandma's great grandpa, John Renfro, had by donating land and building one of the county's first schoolhouses. Uncle Thedford was certainly shiftless and could play the fool when he wanted to. (I suspect he was joshing when he complained about Aunt Addie not turning down his bed covers at night.) He just sort of ambled around through life doing things his way. And therein lies his legacy.

At Uncle Thedford's funeral the preacher distilled this to its essence by saying, "When you saw somebody walking down the street smiling or chuckling to "theirself," you knew for sure they'd just been chatting with Thedford." To my way of thinking, that's a mighty fine way to be remembered.

THEDFORD RUSSELL "WOOING"
A YOUNG LADY

25
Grandma's Favorite Things

She had three: eating ice cream, going to church, and fishing. Her capacity and hankering for ice cream outdid that of most young'uns — with one difference: she did not bite off the bottom of a double dip cone first, so melted goo never leaked down onto her bosom. She ate it before it melted anyway. In the days before refrigerators she could only indulge when she went to town or when we cranked out a freezer of the homemade kind on the iceman's delivery day or when somebody with a car or truck brought out a block of ice. After the backwoods got wired for electricity, she would buy a quart or two, usually vanilla, and put it in the refrigerator freezer, but it got eaten up within a day or two.

As for going to church, when the settlement got left with no place to hold services, Grandma built a church house of her own persuasion, Pentecostal, in the corner of Grandpa's cornfield. Recall from an earlier chapter that once upon a time Oak Flat had a schoolhouse that the various denominations "time shared" for their services. Then, when schools were consolidated into central campuses in local towns, Oak Flat's schoolhouse was moved to Huntington.

The Baptists got busy right quick after this and built a one-room church house painted inside and out. A bona fide sign painter made them a sign they put out front. Randolph and Stella donated the land for it about 15 yards away from their "tank" (that is, stock water pond), one of our favorite swimming holes partly because no one had ever seen a moccasin snake around it.

The Pentecostals then figured they needed a church house of their own too, "they" being mostly Grandma and Sister Emma (pronounced "Emmer"). Sister Emma's reputation in her younger days verged on the scandalous, including — it was said — sneaking off with men at dances to drink whiskey. But later she had been saved. She declared herself a preacher and could preach a Bible-thumping sermon along with the best of them.

I don't know how Grandma persuaded Grandpa to give up a chunk of his cornfield, but he deeded just under an acre over to the Oak Flat Pentecostal Church. Soon thereafter the settlement had another one-room painted church house. The small box-like building with neither plumbing nor electricity required no outside construction labor. Sister Emma's husband, her big strapping son, and Grandpa did the heavy carpentry. A few others, including Grandma, Sister Emma and her younger children, some other Pentecostals, and me, pitched in on the less strenuous stuff.

Building materials couldn't have cost much since lumber was available at cut-rate prices from local sawmills. I have no idea where the money came from, though, except that Sister Emma always seemed to have a wad of bills in her purse. I have a hunch Grandpa also donated the proceeds from selling a cow, although he never uttered a word about it. The one Bible scripture he openly admitted to believing was "never let your left hand know what your right hand is doing."

On several occasions when nails, hinges, and such were needed from town, I got to go get them — all by myself in Sister Emma's car! I lacked a couple of years of being eligible for a driver's license, but Sister Emma would hand me some dollar bills and the car keys. The Chevy, an old stick-shift jalopy, sort of ran the same way I could sort of drive. Since the clutch wouldn't spring back after it had been depressed for shifting, I right quick learned to pull it back to its full upright position with the toe end of my foot. Every time we worked on building the church, I secretly wished that something would be needed from town.

Within a couple of months the church house was finished and painted. But something was missing. It had no sign out front. I guess the money had run out by then because I was nominated to make one. I got ahold of some leftover paint and a nice board on which I lightly outlined the letters. But then I could find only a few old brushes all caked up with dried paint. When nobody offered me cash and car keys to go buy a couple of new ones, I decided I could by-cracky make them myself. I trimmed up some old rags into thin strips then tied them to the ends of two straight sticks. The end result looked like mops for a rustic dollhouse. The finished sign would have looked better if I'd finger-painted it. We nailed it up over the church house door anyway, maybe because of the same sentiment that adults today feel when they display their young'uns' artistic attempts on the door of the fridge.

Sister Emma and Grandma held regular services in the church house for about five years although only a handful of folks ever attended. By then,

Under the Black Gum Tree

Oak Flat had become predominantly Baptist with only a few Pentecostals scattered here and there. The two denominations differ in several ways, notably in the importance Pentecostals place on speaking in tongues. Grandpa never went to church much anyway, but at one point he decided to join Grandma's church. When some staunch Pentecostal leaders found out he had never been moved to speak in tongues, they told him he could attend services but not become a member.

After the church house fell into disuse, somebody outside the family acquired the building and moved it to I don't know where. Today that acre is covered with an impenetrable thicket.

Maybe you've noticed that buildings got moved around a lot in those days. According to one old tale, a family with a pretty good house and a real good well but poor soil for farming bought a bare acreage of better farmland. They moved their house to the new location, then decided they might as well move the well too. So they carefully dug up the well and loaded it onto log rollers. They did get it moved and eased into the new hole they'd dug for it. But somewhere along the way it sprung a leak and never again produced as much water as it had before.

Grandma didn't get to satisfy her urge for fishing very often while Grandpa was alive and, therefore, farming. With all the work around the place they simply had no time for fishing. Grandpa didn't care much for fishing anyway except maybe for "going to the river" for a few days, about the only time except Christmas when unsaved menfolks could get their fill, or more, of liquor. (Grandpa once said that the problem with going to the river was that some damn fool always wanted to fish.)

As a footloose widow, Grandma hung up her milk bucket and got a fishing pole. She knew every spot within a 10-mile radius where fish lurked. With her pole and can of worms she took off on her own to fishing "holes" within walking distance. For those farther away, her older grandchildren soon became very accommodating chauffeurs. Even after the road was paved and the river only 20 minutes or so away by chauffeured vehicle, I don't recall her ever going there. Instead, she fished in creeks, tanks, and borrow pits, many of which held scant water by late summer. But, nevertheless, she often caught a mess of small "fry," usually perch.

We never wonder how fish got into creeks in the first place. On the other hand, folks used to think it mysterious or downright miraculous (many probably still do) that fish got into tanks and borrow pits (slough-like excavations maybe five feet or more deep where dirt has been "borrowed" in order to raise the level of road beds). But somehow these water holes often contain living and reproducing fish that certainly were not stocked by human hands. Some folks said that, when natural streams dried up in a drought, fish eggs would be blown from the gritty bottoms to wetter habitats. Others said fish swam from one water hole to another through underground streams.

When Grandma wanted to get to a promising fishing spot, property lines or fences didn't stop her, a habit her chauffeurs didn't cotton to but went along with anyway. I can still see her gathering the skirt of her Mother Hubbard dress up tight around her legs so she could squeeze through the strands of a barbwire fence. We'd say "Grandma, we're trespassing on so-and-so's property," and she'd say, "That's all right. I know them and they won't care." Some did care. Landowners have long been wary of unannounced visitors traipsing around on their place. Several times, when owners saw us at their tanks, they came over to check things out. But Grandma was right I guess. She did know them, and we'd chat a while. Then they'd say it was okay to fish there.

Once when we had trespassed to get to a family's tank, we caught several "fish-like somethings" about as long as a dollar bill. They looked somewhat like catfish but not quite like any catfish I had ever seen. About this time the farmwife came out to check into the situation. During our chat she told us they had drained the tank a while back and that nothing but "pollywogs" moved back in. I had always thought "pollywog" meant a frog tadpole, but my brother Fred, the wildlife biologist, said some folks used the word to refer to mudcats, a sort of primitive version of the more familiar catfish. Their ancestral look didn't stop Grandma from taking them home for supper.

Getting off on a fishing trip with Grandma was easy. We didn't have to load the trunk with an ice chest and tackle box and the dozen or more other things most fishermen lug off on their expeditions. She carried only her cane pole, already set up with string (not fishing line), hook, sinker, and cork bobber, and of course a can of worms. Getting the worms was easy too. For several years she kept an "earthworm nursery" on a patch of dirt in the yard. From time to time she'd pour some water or coffee grounds on it so it stayed damp. The earthworms did whatever earthworms do to produce more earthworms, and you only had to dig a shovel or two of dirt to pluck out enough to fill the bait can. A few years later Grandma found an even easier way to keep fish bait on hand.

Unlike fancy rod and reel fishermen who feel obliged to frequently invest in the newest artificial lure, bait-can-toting fisherfolks haven't been faced with a choice of newfangled earthworms. Other kinds of bait worms, though, became popular on at least two occasions. In the first half of the last century a Catalpa worm fad swept across the Southern U.S. (and maybe elsewhere). The Catalpa, a fast-growing tree that's covered with clusters of beautiful white blossoms in early summer, becomes infested with a kind of worm that makes a pretty good fish bait. But more important, you can fill your bait can just by shaking the worms off a few limbs. The tree's common names include "Catawber," Fishbait tree, and Cigar tree because its long brown seedpods look somewhat like skinny cigars. Although Grandma never had a Catalpa tree, Aunt Mary did, though for its blossoms rather than for fish bait. Her tree did get full of Catalpa worms in the same mysterious way that fish get into tanks and borrow pits all on their own.

On another occasion, some kind of mealy worm, a fat grub worm about an inch long, became a popular new fish bait. It's called a mealy worm because it can be kept alive in the refrigerator in a coffee can full of damp cornmeal, where it hibernates until warmed up. And, of course, Grandma devoted a whole shelf of her fridge to several canfuls awaiting her next fishing trip.

We all reminisce often on about fishing with Grandma, particularly about how she'd land a fish. Most bait-can-toting fishermen sit down on the bank of the water hole at least sometimes. It used to be said that you could tell when to plant your summer garden by whether these folks fished standing up or sitting down. Until spring had gotten a firm grip on the weather they fished standing up because the still cold ground chilled their behinds. By along about April in our neck of the woods, the ground had warmed up enough to plant black-eyed peas and to sit down to fish. Grandma, however, never, ever fished sitting down.

If Grandma didn't catch a fish within 20 minutes, or 30 at the most, she'd head off to another fishing hole. Maybe she fished standing up so she'd be good'n ready to take off to a more promising spot. A better reason, though, was that she had perfected her own technique for setting the hook and landing the fish in one fell swoop.

Many a fish has been able to swallow the bait without, as the saying goes, swallowing it hook, line, and sinker — or at least without becoming seriously attached to the hook. If you want to catch a fish instead of just messing around with a pole in your hands, you have to set the hook. That is, when the bobber begins to dance around and dip under the surface or you feel a tug on the line, you have to immediately jerk the pole, and hence the line, upward to implant the hook in the fish. Then you figure out how to get the snagged fish out of the water and into your hands.

I never saw Grandma lose a fish by not setting the hook or by failing to land it. Her procedure began the instant the bobber began to dance and go under a dab. In a single motion she'd fling pole, line, and fish with all the force of a golf swing except vertically in an arc up over her head. When the pole reached an angle just past the top of her head she'd let go of it. Then the whole shebang sailed off and landed a good ways behind her. If there had been an Olympic fish-pole-flinging event, Grandma could have covered her walls in gold.

The fish, of course, then had to be retrieved (often a task for us chauffeurs). This was easy at tanks because they are surrounded by bald, open pastures. On the other hand, woods and briars and such grow right up to the banks on at least one side of most creeks and borrow pits. I don't recall that any of us ever had to get a fish out of a tree. But I shall never forget blundering around in a bramble patch to grab a slippery, flouncing fish.

#9 UNDER THE BLACK GUM
SOME CORNY JOKES

THE LAZY MAN: There was once a farmer so lazy he never did a lick of work. He sat in the shade and watched as his tired wife and young'uns plowed as best they could with a skin-and-bones mule. Their crops yielded only a dab more than the seeds they'd been planted with. Folks in the settlement helped them out for a while, but finally got fed up with the lazy man. Then they all got together and decided that, for all the good he was doing, they might as well go bury him. So they went over and loaded him in a wagon and headed off to the graveyard. On their way a stranger came by and asked what they were doing. After they told him, the stranger allowed as how that, if they all chipped in a good bit, it might convince the man that he needed to get to work. They thought about it, and one man decided he could take the family 25 bushels of corn. Another said he could too, and another chimed in with 50 bushels. At this, the stranger asked the lazy man if all this corn would make him change his ways. To which, the lazy man asked, "Is the corn shelled?" When his neighbors said no, the man replied, "Then just drive on."

GOING FISHING WITH THREE MATCHES: Once, during the lull after their crops were laid by in the early summer, some farmers decided "to go to the river," that is, to go camp out on the river and fish. So they loaded up a wagon with quilts for sleeping pallets, a few pots, pans, fishing lines and such. The trip to the river took several hours. About halfway there it occurred to one man to ask who'd brought the matches. It turned out that only one man had matches, and he had only three. After they'd ridden on a ways, one of the men brought up the possibility that the matches might not light up. So, another man had the bright idea that they ought to strike one to see if it would light up. It lit up fine. After another little ways, one of them said, "We've only got two matches left. What if they won't light up?" So they struck another match and sure enough it too lit up. Now they were in a swivet about the status of the last match. One of the men opined that the only way to find out was to strike it, which they did. It, too, lit up just fine.

THE FARMER AND THE AG AGENT: Once a young graduate from agricultural college with all sorts of new ideas about how to farm got a job as the government's Ag Agent. His rounds of the local farms included one owned by a man who had farmed it for years and years. On his visits, the Ag Agent would always advise the old farmer of a better way to do one thing or another. The old farmer, of course, kept doing things the way he always had. The Ag Agent finally lost his patience and blurted out to the old farmer: "If you'd do what I tell you, you could farm twice as good as you do now." The farmer answered, "Hell, I ain't farming half as good as I know how to already."

26
The Great Dispersal

People welcomed the New Year of 1942 with trepidation and optimism as the news yo-yoed between bleak accounts of Axis victories to hopeful reports of Allied progress overseas. The Japanese captured Singapore and Java, invaded Burma, and forced the Bataan Death March. The Nazis reached Stalingrad in Russia, and Hitler began the Holocaust. On the optimistic side, General Jimmy Doolittle bombed Tokyo, and Americans took Midway and won the Battle of the Coral Sea.

The public heard nary a word though, at least for several years, about two historic developments of WWII. The Germans began working on the V-2 rocket, and Enrico Fermi and his team at the University of Chicago split the atom (an early step on the road to the atomic bomb). Folks *had* heard that Disney's *Bambi* would soon be playing at a picture show near them. By the end of '42, "White Christmas" was played about as often as "Silent Night."

On the home front, rationing began early on with sugar and gasoline on the list for starters. Women — and men who weren't off in the military — began leaving the hinterlands to work in "defense plants." Rosie the Riveters were in demand all over the country, including at shipyards where welders instead would later be needed.

On battlefronts worldwide, shipments of everything from tanks and cannons to bullets and K-rations were delayed due to a shortage of cargo ships. So Henry Kaiser figured out a quicker way of building what became known as Liberty ships. He is probably remembered best today, if at all, as founder of the Kaiser Permanente HMO. But back then he was already rich and well known for his cement company, which among other accomplishments was one of the primary builders of Boulder Dam. And, he owned several shipyards.

Welding had been around a good while by then but the technology wasn't advanced enough to hold big structures together, so ship's hulls, skyscraper girders, and so forth were riveted into place. Kaiser and his team improved welding techniques and equipment to handle big, heavy stuff, thus shaving off the time and cost of building a ship by nearly a third. By the end of '43, shipyards were turning out three new welded Liberty ships per day. This didn't completely phase out jobs for Rosies back then but, in the years since, welding has almost completely replaced riveting.

On our own home front, in 1942 the Lufkin Foundry began manufacturing cannon barrels in addition to oil pumping units. Almost overnight a high chain-link fence with guardhouses surrounded its premises, and all employees had to wear picture badges. This could have put a crimp into my stopping by to see Daddy on my way home from school.

In those days two main traffic lanes ran from a back gate through the inside of the Foundry's plant and to an entrance to the office building. Piles of metal material to be smelted were stacked alongside the lane closest to the plant's outer wall. The innermost lane ran alongside the smelting furnaces where this metal was smelted down to be poured into casting molds.

The Foundry sat about halfway between our house and my school, all within easy walking distance of each other. In the olden days young'uns walked back and forth to school on their own, although I do recall someone walking with me directly from home to school the first few times to make sure I knew the way. Also, by then, I had tagged along enough with Daddy on his rounds at work to know my way up and down these two lanes in the Foundry.

In the days before picture badges, the back gate must have stayed open a lot, or so it seems in my recollections. At any rate, I do recollect moseying through it and proceeding on to the office building from time to time. Except for once, I took the outer lane where the metal was stored, and I marveled at how high it was stacked and took in the scene in general. Employees were around and probably kept an eye on me, but nobody stopped me. They recognized me and made chitchat such as, "Goin' to see your Daddy?" When I got to the engineering office, Daddy would greet me and sit me down at a little low table he had fixed up for me, complete with some cast-off drafting instruments, beside his big drafting board. And I would sit there and draw circles with the compass and lines with the straight edge until I decided it was time to go on home.

The outer lane past all the stacked metal was no more hazardous than a busy aisle at today's Home Depots, and a lot quieter and less congested. The inner lane past the furnaces would certainly be declared hazardous today. The decibel level from the furnaces and the exhaust fans in the roof above them meant you could sort of be heard if you yelled (like at a modern Rock concert). A thick odor of oil and grease and hot metal filled the air. And, of course, the area was hotter all year than Texas ever gets in July. All that made it a scary place, and I remember hanging onto Daddy's hand when I went through there with him. One day, however, I got brave.

I went through the back gate as usual, and for reasons unknown took the inner lane (maybe the Devil told me to do it). I walked carefully down the middle of the lane as Daddy always did, all the while feeling euphoric and grown up. That feeling is still burned into my memory (pun probably intended). When I got to the office, I casually announced that I had taken the inside lane. Daddy just humphed and sat me down at my little drafting table.

The picture badge edict did not put a crimp in my after-school detours. I don't know how it came to happen, but one day Daddy took me to the badge picture-taker, who later presented me with a badge. It only contained my name and picture, but the guards at the gates would look at it and smile, then wave me through. Maybe they thought I was an Engineer-in-Training.

In the late summer of 1942 we joined what has been dubbed the Great Dispersal when Daddy signed on with an engineering outfit in Houston. We had to rent a house there but, because flocks of other folks had also dispersed to Houston, finding a decent, affordable house was about like trying to find a hen's nest in a blackberry patch. We settled on a "mansion" complete with a real basement, a dumbwaiter, and a big third-floor dormer room. In order to pay the rent, Mama took in boarders. The house was only a few blocks from the Dental College, and three dental students moved into the dormer room before we finished unpacking.

By then lots of things had been rationed, including meat, coffee, and sugar, so Mama had to scramble to come up with passable menus. I remember sweetening Ovaltine, and occasionally coffee, with corn syrup and even eating some of the frequently served brains and eggs. The once-a-week tongue entrée was okay if I thought of it as ham, which it does taste like. Even with gasoline rationing we somehow managed trips back to the Piney Woods fairly often and would return with a carload of vegetables and meat that Grandma and Grandpa had raised. Usually the country folks didn't need anything from Houston that we could take in exchange. One occasion, however, does stand out in my mind.

Most seed supplies had bypassed the Piney Woods in favor of the larger farms elsewhere that grew edibles for the military. So, when planting time rolled around and Grandpa could find only a pitiful few corn seed locally, he asked Mama to see what she could find in Houston. She located a seed store a couple of blocks off Main Street right smack in downtown Houston. I went with her and recall a no-frills, poorly lit store lined with seed bins. She bought two big sacks of corn seed, and we took them to Grandpa a few days later. He was proud of them but remarked that they weren't the "Hastings Prolific" variety he usually planted, but that they'd work out fine.

We lived in Houston for two years, but less than one in the "mansion," or anywhere else. In what became routine, the landlord sold the house and we had to find another. All told we lived in four houses, each smaller and more affordable than the one before.

I remember these years as exciting. Dozens of our kinfolks had also migrated to Houston, so we had an ongoing string of family get-togethers. One cousin's Louisiana-style shrimp boils became especially popular. Daddy drank almost not at all, and Mama not much more, but some grownups learned that beer went better at these shindigs than iced tea.

We all looked forward to these get-togethers, but some of us were equally attracted to a low-budget kiddie carnival out on South Main. It had no snack bar and only three rides: a merry-go-round (that is, "hobby horses"), a carousel with little kiddie cars, and *real live ponies*!

The 20 or so ponies ranged from pint-sized Shetlands to a few taller than I was. The little bitty ponies carrying little bitty young'uns circled the inner track in slow motion. At the other end of the scale, the larger ponies rounded the outer track lickety- split. I always chose the very fastest one, even if it meant my ride would be over in short order. A ride cost a nickel and I, for one, saved every coin I could beg or earn. On one memorable day I had saved up a dollar's worth of rides. It plumb tuckered out the pony, but I would have kept going if I'd had more nickels.

On the other side of the coin, so to speak, a couple of scary situations occurred while we lived in Houston. In 1943 a polio (or infantile paralysis) epidemic tore across the whole country. Researchers were working on a vaccine against the polio virus, but it took another 14 years to develop. This virus does its damage by rendering muscles useless, including the ones we use to breathe. If the infection does not work its way to the respiratory system, victims can survive but are usually left crippled (think Franklin D. Roosevelt). Back then, patients with infections affecting respiration were transferred, if possible, to often overloaded facilities with iron lungs.

The iron lung, an early version of the mechanical respirator, was a big sealed cylinder that entombed all but the patient's head. Its internal pressure alternated to compress the patient's chest thus inflating the lungs, then to relax the pressure thus causing the lungs to exhale. In other words, it functions somewhat like the artificial respiration we were taught to apply after we'd rescued a drowning swimmer.

No one in our connection caught polio but we'd all heard of someone's relative off somewhere in an iron lung, and that so-and-so was crippled because of infantile paralysis. Besides being scared of it, the only effect on us, and particularly the young'uns, was that swimming pools shut down for a while because it was thought they spread polio germs.

The other scary situation involved a serial rapist stalking the woods surrounding several Houston parks. This hit closer to home than polio had since he targeted a park where we occasionally picnicked. I'd never heard of a rapist before and didn't know what it all meant, so I figured it was sort of like an escaped convict on the loose (maybe it was). We still went to parks in well-chaperoned groups, but this introduction to urban crime led us to make doubly sure all our doors were locked at night.

Throughout our time in Houston it became increasingly clear we were winning the war. In 1943 the Allies invaded Italy, which later surrendered, and we drove the Nazis out of North Africa. In the Pacific we captured Guadalcanal and New Guinea and won the Battle of the Bismarck Sea. In Eastern Europe the Russians just about annihilated the German army at Stalingrad. Air strikes by both friend and foe intensified, including German air raids on London, which escalated to V-1 and later V-2 "buzz bomb" attacks, and Allied bombing raids over Germany. While all this was going on, we sang "Coming in on a Wing and a Prayer" and "Mairzy Doats." The musical *Oklahoma* won a Pulitzer Prize and *Casablanca* an Academy Award.

"Don't Fence Me In" made the popular music hit parade in 1944. Its words symbolize, to me anyway, the country's determination to bust back barriers and keep on going, as probably best demonstrated by D-Day and the Battle of the Bulge. All the while, at places like Quebec, Malta, etc., the "Big Three" or "Big Four" (some combination of Roosevelt, Churchill, Stalin, Mme. Chiang Kai Shek, Mackenzie King of Canada) met to decide on new alliances and boundaries in the coming postwar world. (In some cases, such as agreeing to divide up Korea, they "built fences" where none had existed before.)

In June of 1944 we were living in our fourth and last house in Houston.

At that time, almost everyone, including a good many young'uns, knew D-Day would happen soon, but that's all. In keeping with the posters all over the place warning that "loose lips sink ships," the hundreds, if not thousands of government and military officials involved in D-Day planning kept their lips zipped. The planned date and place of landing in France was probably one of the best-kept secrets in World history.

June 6, 1944, D-Day. I remember that hot summer day. The asphalt paving on our street had melted into hot tar puddles. Grownups in our family and millions of others across the country and beyond packed churches for prayer vigils. With all the wartime secrecy and censorship, families did not know whether their relatives and friends serving in Europe were part of the Normandy invasion.

My memories of the War are those of a child: eating brains and eggs, riding the ponies, learning the words of "Mairzie Doats." I was either unaware or could not grasp the depth of the fear, anxiety, and heartbreak many adults coped with. Lots of our kinfolks and friends served along with the roughly 16 million other Americans during the war. Military casualties numbered about 400 thousand killed and over 600 thousand wounded. As with the polio epidemic and the rapist in the park, we were spared direct experience of this. All the GIs in our connection came back in one piece.

Some U.S. civilian casualties occurred, for instance among civilians working overseas. But we also got off scot-free compared to other countries, both friend and foe, such as England, Russia, China, Japan, and Germany. Most civilians in the U.S. never looked into the eyes of an enemy combatant. That is, except for some folks in the hinterlands.

Along about the middle of World War II, the government converted the fairgrounds at Lufkin into a prisoner of war camp for captured Germans. A fenced-in tent city complete with barracks, a mess hall, etc., covered a sizeable section of the grounds. To either earn their keep or pay for their sins, the POWs were put to work clearing underbrush in the National Forests in the area. They were loaded into the backs of Army trucks to go to and from the work sites, all the while under the scrutiny of armed guards.

The Angelina National Forest surrounded a good portion of Grandpa's cornfield, as well as the land of neighboring farmers. On many occasions the prisoners worked right up to the field fences, and the farmers struck up conversations with them in broken English. Once, while Grandpa was plowing, a big coachwhip snake dashed out from the underbrush the prisoners were clearing and tore out under the fence into the cornfield.

This skin of this snake, a racer type, has a pattern that looks somewhat like the braided pattern of a laced-leather whip. Grandpa yelled to the prisoners in his most authoritarian tone to catch it and take it back where it came from. Since coachwhips are harder to catch than a scared Tomcat, bedlam broke out as prisoners and snake zipped around the field like somebody had pushed all their fast-forward buttons. After a dab of zipping, they caught on to the prank.

The guards took a mellow view of such things. Once a neighboring family took several of the prisoners over to their place for dinner (at noon). This didn't bother the guards but some folks in the settlement allowed as how talking to the prisoners was fine, but it'd be risky to invite them into the house. Another time, a prisoner got left behind when the guards loaded the truck to go back to the fairgrounds. When he realized the truck had left without him, he walked every step of the 15 miles back to camp.

When Daddy's vacation came around in the summer of 1944, we took off to a "tourist cabin" near Corpus Christi for our usual round of fishing and swimming. But, on this trip, we fished and swam less often. I wondered about this and soon learned that Daddy was job hunting. His job in Houston hadn't panned out, and we all felt Corpus would be a fine place to live. We had dispersed once then lived all over Houston, so we were used to moving. By the time vacation was over, Daddy had a new job. After all, dispersing is a lot like eating peanuts. It's hard to stop with just one.

Leah and Eli's family; Christmas 1939 in front of Fred & Lillian's house in Lufkin. Our last Christmas there before we joined the Great Dispersal. Beginning at right, standing: Lillian Graham holding Linwood, Leah Russell, Mary and Kyle Hawkins, Eli Russell, Jewel and Dale Russell; Young'uns in front: Billie Jo Hawkins, Winnie Graham, and Fred Jr.

27
Some More Peanuts

In moving to Corpus Christi in the late summer of 1944 we had left the black-eyed pea/pinto bean divide many miles behind. We no longer had kinfolks behind every tree, although Mama did manage to track down a few. And besides, the trees were mesquites instead of pines. We made friends, including some from so far away that we thought of them as Yankees. The news media had lumped us all into "Yanks" anyway. With the war at its peak, the headlines daily announced one "Yank" victory after another and Allied victories also. Again our isolation from the front lines shielded us from many effects of the war, but we did rub elbows with hundreds of "Yanks" being trained at the Naval Air Stations around Corpus. We got to know several sailors and pilots, some of whom really did come from Northern climes.

We spent two happy years in Corpus. We fished and swam, of course, and also enjoyed the oleander and bougainvillea that bloomed almost year round. And Daddy liked his new job.

In Houston he'd been working on a newfangled combination heating/cooling unit. The project had gotten bogged down in a snarl of problems that convinced Daddy the unit could not be built with the technology then available, and he liked to see the finished product of his designs. In his new job at a chemical plant in Corpus, he had plenty to design and got to oversee construction.

Toward the end of the war technological advances of a new and different kind began popping up like collard greens in February. Although many had been in the making for years, most folks didn't know pea turkey about what they were or how they worked (and many folks still don't). This "new" technology dealt with stuff like atoms and electrons you couldn't see even under a microscope.

In 1943, in England, Alan Turing designed a computing device to unscramble German codes. The next year IBM came out with another computer-type machine, the Mark I. It used vacuum tubes the size of light bulbs and was too specialized to pass for what we know as a general-purpose computer. That "real" computer, the ENIAC, came out in 1945, again built with vacuum tubes as were all computers for about the next 12 years.

Besides being about the same size as light bulbs, vacuum tubes give off roughly the same amount of heat and burn out regularly. With its hundreds of tubes, an early computer and its required air-conditioning system took up a gymnasium-sized room. Another electronic marvel that would streamline all this had been developed, but it didn't become available for general use until the late 1950s.

Bell Labs, the research arm of the Bell Telephone System, announced the invention of the transistor in 1947. For several years before that, engineers here and there had gotten hold of early versions of these semiconductors to play around with. Two years before Bell Lab's announcement, our friend Tom, a Navy pilot, snitched one from the base and showed it to us. It was the size, and looked pretty much like, a .22 caliber cartridge and could replace one vacuum tube. Semiconductor devices have now been miniaturized so much that the earlier gymnasium-sized computer innards can be packed into laptops, cell phones, and such.

We celebrated the end of the war, sort of, during our second year in Corpus. The official proclamation of victory in Europe, V-E Day on May 8, 1945, came as an anti-climax to events of the previous weeks after the Allies had closed in on both sides of Berlin. Hitler had committed suicide on April 30th and, two days later, Berlin surrendered to the Russians. All the while the Allies racked up victory after victory in the Pacific, but we were still at war with Japan. And it could have gone on for who knows how long except for the new science and technology of small particles.

In July of 1945, the world first heard of the atom bomb after a test explosion at White Sands, New Mexico. I recall it being the main topic of conversation as people tried to comprehend its power. Tom the pilot tried to explain how powerful it was, but nobody could explain why. I asked Tom if they had any of those bombs at the Naval Base, and he answered, "Why, of course not." Right or wrong, Hiroshima was bombed on August 6th and Nagasaki three days later. Japan surrendered on the 14th.

When Germany and then Japan surrendered, we felt jubilacious but didn't go out and dance in the streets or beat on pot lids like some people did. Neither did we gloat over our victory. The killing had stopped and an era of world peace, we were assured, was at hand.

The following spring we bought a place on the outskirts of Corpus on a lot large enough for a horse, which I had been agitating for. The house needed work, but Daddy looked forward to fixing it up. Even before the remodeling got underway, we bought Nellie, a gray mare that'd been retired from working cattle.

We would have been all set to enjoy the expected era of world peace except that Daddy's health started failing. Skin problems he'd dealt with for several years began flaring up viciously; also, arthritis began poking up its ugly head. The doctors tried various remedies that didn't work. One tried "bathing" his skin with X-rays, which made things worse. The dust at the chemical plant, while not the culprit, was certainly an accomplice.

Oyster shells dredged up in the bay were processed into caustic soda (a version of lye) at the plant for use in cleansers. The plant did not spew out caustic dust all over the place, but more seeped out than anyone would put up with today.

The chemical company had started building a plant in Lake Charles, Louisiana, to produce chlorine gas from salt brine, again for cleansers and also disinfectants. A cadre of engineers, accountants, and such from Corpus was selected to design and operate the new plant. In the fall of 1946, when the company held out the relocation peanut jar to Daddy, he helped himself to one. We couldn't imagine living anywhere but Texas but, on the other hand, Lake Charles was closer than Corpus to the Piney Woods. And, the new plant would be dust free.

We lived in Lake Charles for the next ten years. Throughout that time, as well as our years in Corpus, we still thought of the Piney Woods as "home" and visited there often. My brothers and I spent every summer with Grandma and Grandpa and earned our keep helping out. My brother Fred learned to plow; I helped thin and fertilize corn; we picked black-eyed peas and harvested sweet potatoes. And, of course, we always went to church with Grandma. We also fished in the creek and slipped off to go swimming in the tank. Before we jumped in, we'd check for water moccasins and chase off the hogs that were wallowing in the muddy banks. This clandestine swimming never made us sick and may have bulked up our immune systems.

When we moved from Corpus, we hauled "Nellie Horsie" in a borrowed horse trailer to Grandpa's. He had 30 or 40 head of cattle in those days and used her to gently work them. I sometimes helped him on Nellie, and he rode his skittish gray mare. I had dubs on Nellie, though, and just she and I often roamed around in the woods all day while I sang "hillbilly" songs and smoked stolen cigarettes.

We, as well as a bunch of our dispersed kinfolks, had always figured we'd move back to the Piney Woods someday. And some of us did.

Shortly after the war, a wave of dispersees in our family, mostly cousins, became welders, pipe fitters, and such on the worldwide construction-job circuit. Some of these dispersees later became returnees, although fewer came back than went out. Many of them, especially retirees, had some money in the bank, so they could live wherever they wanted to. Some chose to build modern houses in the Piney Woods; others to live elsewhere. Some who had always figured they'd return someday did, but not to live in modern houses. They made their last trip to the Piney Woods to join our predecessors at Jonesville Cemetery.

28
A Visit to Jonesville

If you drive down almost any back road in Texas, you'll see frequent signs pointing to such and such a family cemetery. In the Piney Woods they're usually several hundred feet off the road on a dirt or gravel lane back in the woods. Nowadays, most are kept weeded and mowed but beyond that their state of repair varies. Those where families chip in to pay a caretaker stay pretty well spruced up; others look downright forlorn. All of them date back at least a century so that inscriptions on eroded tombstone surfaces are difficult, if not impossible, to read. Original wooden grave markers have long since crumbled and in some cases been replaced with new ones.

The graveyard workings of yore, where folks got together to rejuvenate the area and just generally socialize, sing, and eat a big dinner (at noon), have been superseded at some cemeteries by an annual reunion. The work has been done beforehand, so the older folks spend the time trading news and the younger ones meeting kinfolks they've never seen before. Some of us in our family go to these events, but most of us just "drop in" at the cemetery the way we'd just drop in on any of our kinfolks.

Grandma's early predecessors are buried in forlorn cemeteries across the river in San Augustine County. Most of them have faded from memory, so we seldom visit those cemeteries. Our departed who still live on in our memories are buried at Jonesville in Angelina County. We all drop in on them from time to time. We don't wallow in mournful thoughts on these occasions. They all left pleasant memories, even the few who left us before they should have. Well over half of them stayed hale and hearty beyond their three score and ten years, including several who made it into their 80s and 90s. So we reminisce and laugh about their shenanigans and the lighter moments in their lives.

Any visit to Jonesville has to include a stop at the graves of James Eason Russell and his legal wife Caroline (my great-great grandparents). He died at 79 and she at 68. Recall that an inscribed petrified log spans their side-by-side graves.

Grandma Wade is buried at Jonesville, but none of her husbands are. She died at age 90, folks said from cancer but that's not certain because she was only sick a few weeks. When she was in her 80s and living by herself in an apartment in Nacogdoches, she took to riding around town with her grandson Tucker on his motorcycle. During World War II, Tucker (Aunt Cora's son) served in Europe and managed to smuggle a German Army motorcycle back home with him. For several years after that he'd go pick up Grandma Wade of an afternoon. She'd climb on behind him (no, it didn't have a side car) and off they'd go.

Grandpa and Grandma lie side by side at Jonesville. Even though he lived to 77, he'd been taken away too soon according to his myriad friends and kinfolks. It seemed like over half the country turned out to pay their respects at his funeral. On that afternoon every store in town except one closed down. I think he would have felt humbled but also sorry that he couldn't sit up and crack a joke for all those folks.

Grandpa was active until almost the very end. A couple of weeks or so before he got sick I watched as he tried to bulldog a cow the way they do at rodeos. (That is, you grab it by the horns, brace with your feet, and twist its neck until you flip it flat down on the ground.) He wanted to pen up a stubborn old cow but she had other ideas. When she began skittering around, he got mad and grabbed her by the horns. He had a good hold on her horns, but she took off running before he could brace and twist her head. The two of them proceeded thusly for a good 40 feet. Then, when she jumped over a hump in the ground, Grandpa lost his hold and went tumbling off in the other direction. The cow moseyed off contentedly.

About six weeks before he died, Grandpa got so laid low by something that he could barely stand up. He had never been sick a day in his life before and, early on, Aunt Mary said to him, "Papa, this is the first time I've ever seen you in bed in the daytime except for a hangover." He smiled a dab. At first malaria was suspected, but quinine didn't help. Then he "confessed" that while roaming around in the woods a little while earlier he had scooped up a drink of water from the creek in his hat. When the doctors heard this, they immediately diagnosed typhoid and sent Grandpa to the hospital in Lufkin.

It soon became obvious that Grandpa did not have typhoid, but in those days before CT scans and MRIs the doctors had nothing more to base a diagnosis on. It could have been cancer, but we'll never know. He left us many memories. One we often recall goes back to an early morning when it looked like a tornado was about to hit.

In the olden days of open range, Grandpa always turned his team out to graze in the woods at night, and they would come back at breakfast time for their ration of corn. On this particular morning the dead calm air and black clouds warned of a possible tornado (it didn't materialize, but anyway. . .). Also Grandpa's horses had not showed up, and they either didn't hear or ignored his loud whistles. Grandma and Grandpa worried about the tornado and the horses silently until finally she said, "Eli, there hasn't been a leaf stirred this morning." Then he said, "No, nor a horse stirred either." (Read this out loud if you have to.)

Grandma died at age 92, and as with many of our other kinfolks was sick for only a few weeks. She had a heart attack (proving that a multi-year diet of black-eyed peas and turnip greens boiled with salt pork doesn't necessarily doom you to an early demise). She might have made it longer, but was put in a nursing home to recuperate, where she fell and broke her hip. She went downhill from there. Grandma outlived Grandpa by over 20 years, during which she lived in three different places.

She stayed on in the old homestead for a while. It still had the old wood burning cook stove and no indoor plumbing except for water piped from a cistern to a kitchen sink. The fireplace was usable, but Grandma had sworn off messing with fire wood anymore than she had to and tried to keep the place warm with a couple of butane heaters. Uncle Dale had moved a fairly good house (another house moving) to within hollering distance of his own and he got her situated in it. A few years later she got a hankering to be closer to town and rented a house about a mile outside of Huntington. The third place, an apartment in government subsidized housing, was right smack in the middle of town.

Grandma had raised many a garden as a necessity but had pretty much put it in the same category as toting firewood until she moved to the "project." Her apartment had a shirt-tail-sized bare front yard of brick-hard compacted dirt. She didn't want it to look so plug ugly, but knew it wouldn't grow anything as it was. So she went in cahoots on a load of topsoil with a friend who lived across town. Now she clearly couldn't have her share of the soil dumped in front of the project, so it was all unloaded over at her friend's house.

Grandma got a wheelbarrow and pushed it back and forth across town every day (except Sunday) until she'd gotten her half of the topsoil spread on her front yard. The end result — a mass of hollyhocks, marigolds, zinnias, okra, and tomatoes — brightened up her spot in the project.

When the wheelbarrow pushing was going on (she was in her late 80's), I asked her if that wasn't hard, heavy work. She said, "No, once you get the wheelbarrow loaded and lifted up on its wheel, it's easy to push."

Unlike some other kinfolks, neither Mama nor Daddy lived to a ripe old age and both were sick a good while. Daddy died first at the relatively youngish age of 67. The skin problems and arthritis he had coped with for several years got worse and worse until, at age 65, he was forced to retire. Mama had told me much earlier he once said he wouldn't live long after he retired. He lived another two years.

On his death certificate the doctor stated Aplastic Anemia, and I guess that could be right. Recall that another doctor once bathed his skin in X-rays to "cure" his skin problems. I think, though, that two other diseases are also candidates. One is Psoriatic Arthropathy, a combination of flaking skin and aching joints. The other, Lyme Disease, had not been "discovered" and named back then. Daddy had always said his skin problems started with tick bites he'd gotten on a hunting trip. Maybe some combination or none of these is correct. At any rate, treatments from several doctors over these years did no good.

Mama's life spanned only 59 years with just eight of them after Daddy died. During the first six of those she did her best to live a new life of widowhood but then began to feel run down and tired. She was soon diagnosed with intestinal cancer. She had surgery and the early type of chemotherapy available then, but the cancer soon came back. We all know what that means.

During Daddy's last years of bad health, Mama saw the handwriting on the wall and, besides, expenses had skyrocketed. She couldn't go back to teaching full time because her old teaching certificate from Normal College was no longer valid. She could substitute in public schools, though, and also taught a couple of years at a Catholic school that had less stringent requirements than public schools. She also started back to college at McNeese in Lake Charles to get a degree in education. She took classes nights and summers and looked forward to the day when Daddy would somehow make it to her graduation. Maybe he did in a sense. She always said she thought he did. She had one more year of classes to finish when he died.

If she had wanted to up and quit at that point she kept it to herself. In 1954, Lillian marched down the aisle in cap and gown at a full-fledged graduation ceremony (a year before I did likewise).

Mama had six healthy years after Daddy died and, including going to college, packed a lot into them. After graduating she taught lower elementary classes in a rural school just north of Lake Charles. I took a job in Corpus Christi when I graduated, and Mama and my brothers joined me there a year later. She again taught lower elementary classes. When she found she had a knack for teaching the mentally retarded (as they were called in those days), she took more classes and got a certificate in Special Education. She even went by train to a Special Ed conference in Phoenix, the farthest away from the Piney Woods she had ever been.

Mama didn't let all this studying and working interfere with her socializing. When she taught at the little country school, she got so involved with the community that she even went to the basketball games (the school was too small for a football team). The parents of her pupils adored her and they often visited back and forth. She still found time to play bridge, belong to a garden club, and play golf occasionally.

Mama might have been a wizard at managing her time, but she managed her money as though there was no tomorrow. She did keep her checkbook balanced, frequently by borrowing from Peter to pay quite a few Pauls — often with one of us young'uns playing the part of Peter. As a cousin once said, "When Fred was able to work, he bought Lillian anything she wanted," so I think she just couldn't give up that way of life. She had a batch of department store credit cards that she used lavishly — often, I must point out, to buy presents for friends and kinfolks. My brothers and I routinely chipped in on family expenses beginning with our baby-sitting and lawn-mowing earnings back when Daddy's health started downhill. During Mama's last years, when my brother Fred and I had regular incomes (and expenses), we chipped in more serious amounts. But, as the bill collectors got closer and closer to the door, we just about got petered out.

From a country girl born into a bare-bones house with no indoor plumbing and nothing powered by electrons, Mama's relatively short life spanned an eventful period. She grew up without even a radio or telephone, but lived until folks all over had at least one of each plus a refrigerator and a TV. When she was 17, women in the United States got the right to vote. She lived during the flu epidemic, two World Wars, and the development of the atomic bomb. The Space Program was well underway during her last years, but she didn't make it long enough to watch TV coverage of astronauts on the moon. She was born the year of the first successful airplane flight at Kitty Hawk, but flew in a plane only once.

Throughout Mama's last days she somehow stayed optimistic, at least outwardly. She went on disability leave from the Corpus school system her last year and, for the first time since we had dispersed, reminisced about the Piney Woods. She talked of moving back to a modern house somewhere around Lufkin and asked us to help her get there. Her condition ruled out a car trip, so we chartered a small plane with a seat that folded into a sort of gurney. Brother Fred went with her. When they landed, an ambulance took her directly to the Lufkin hospital to rest and get IVs enough to build her up for the next step. That next step, two weeks later, was to Jonesville.

Lillian was survived by a horde of kinfolks including two siblings (Uncle Dale and Aunt Mary) and a still-hale-and-hearty mother. And three grown young'uns who, in spite of the casual way she'd raised them, turned out pretty good.

#10 UNDER THE BLACK GUM
MAMA'S WORDS OF WISDOM

During my growing up years, Mama went along with the prevailing view that sparing the rod spoiled the child. She would never have used a rod of course. For minor offenses a spanking by hand was sufficient; something really "aggervating" required "whupping my butt" with a switch yanked off the nearest bush. My brothers mostly escaped such corrective measures, but not because they did no wrong. They did a lot that I thought they should get their butts whupped for. Mama always said she raised all three of us differently, and for some reason she applied the "rod" sparingly with them. Whether they're spoiled and I'm not is open to question.

But if Mama could whup my butt, and sometimes my brothers' (and fuss at us), she was a model of diplomacy in her dealings with others. She put great stock into keeping peace with everybody and followed her own set of ground rules to avoid stirring up trouble. Except for a couple of occasions, I don't remember exactly why she whupped my butt. I do recall some of these words of wisdom that she passed on to me. Take them for what they're worth in this day and age.

Don't ever criticize, find fault, or say a bad word about a person's kinfolks to that person. He or she might agree with you, often without saying so, but will take your words as personal affront and get mad at you.

If your young'uns get into a squabble with other young'uns, don't say a word about it to the other's parents. More often than not they'll take it as an insult and stay mad at you long after the young'uns have settled their differences.

Don't ever even go out on a first date with someone you wouldn't want to bring home to meet the family. You never know what the first date's going to lead to, so don't start down that road if it could lead to problems.

Don't carry on to other folks about your operation(s), rheumatism, and such. You'll only bore them, and besides they might have a more serious aliment than you do.

Mama always told us if we ever got a paddling (or whuppin') at school, we'd get another one when we got home. I took this with a grain of salt since girls were always "spared the rod" at school. If my brothers ever had to bend over and gird their loins for the paddle, they kept quiet about it. I'm pretty sure she would have ignored this rule if she thought the punishment had been unfair because, on the other hand, Mama said we could always count on her no matter what we did. She said she might not always approve, but we were her young'uns and she'd never deny us her support if we needed it.

29
A Cabin in the Woods

Not much farming goes on in the Piney Woods anymore. Many farms of the olden days have been carved up into smaller plots and sold to retirees and folks who work at regular jobs in the area. Some have been parceled up for the descendants of the early settlers who, like me, inherited a plot of the "old homestead," with each plot becoming successively smaller as the land was passed along to each subsequent generation (my plot is 6 acres). Affluent people in various cities have bought a few quite large spreads and intend to someday subdivide them for "country estates."

Most of these Piney Woodsians, both new and old, keep at least vestiges of the old farming traditions going. Some raise small herds of cattle as a sideline. Many keep saddle horses for pleasure riding. Some folks grow hay for their own feed supply or to sell. There are a few bona fide cattle ranches here and there with large herds, and processing plants in the area buy chickens by the thousands from some hardworking souls. And lots of folks grow gardens with okra, collards, "roast'nears," and – yes – black-eyed peas.

Logging is still big business, and many of yesteryear's fields and pasturelands have now become tree farms. Clear cutting, where every smidgen of timber is hauled off to the mill or left behind as slash, has been replaced by selective cutting. When this is done right – and sometimes it isn't – a forester, preferably a certified one, goes through the timber stand and marks each tree to be cut with a stripe of bright paint.

Cuttings are done every five to ten years, so besides marking the trees to be taken on "this cut," a major aim is to prepare the stand for the next cut. Large trees that shadow smaller ones get a spray of paint. Others destined for a paint stripe include those with forked crotches that could split and fall, and those with growing limbs that will interfere with the growth of their brethren that are to remain. This creates a well-spaced and well-formed stand of timber beneath which other kinds of vegetation such as muscadine and yellow jasmine vines, redbud trees, yaupon bushes, and wildflowers spring up and take hold. The end result is that you can see both the forest and the trees.

Along with the memory of farmers plowing their fields with horse and mule teams, the dog-trot style of house has joined the realm of nostalgia. A few of these may have been restored or duplicated here and there, but nowadays most folks live in modern "homes." A lot of updated small (and painted) houses – two rooms wide and three long with front porch and back stoop – from the 1940s era still dot the landscape, along with newer to brand-new houses. Some of these "homes" with affluent owners are downright palatial. Most are more like what you'd find in middle-class city neighborhoods. Many are brick and hence unpainted.

Where once houses were lit, if they were lit at all, by candles then, later, by coal oil lamps, folks nowadays get the Internet and cable or dish TV. Where once it took folks an hour to get to town in the wagon (and they didn't go every Saturday of a month), United Parcel and FedEx make regular deliveries. And, instead of sending for the doctor or making do without in an emergency, you now can dial 911. Lufkin has become a city – a small one, but nevertheless a city – where you can find everything you need and most things you want.

Yet, despite all these changes, much remains the same. Pinto beanish things have crept in, but the black-eyed pea culture still prevails. Folks still eat dinner at noon and kick the "tars" on a new car they'd like to buy. Most still call their parents Mama and Daddy. There are still many locally owned stores, and some of them close on Sunday. Some menfolks, especially the newer ones, think they have to wear cowboy boots – usually ones that have never been sullied by stepping in a cow patty. But blue denim "Uncle Jack" overalls far outnumber cowboy boots.

Some of the settlements out in the hinterlands have dried up, but many others are still populated, albeit sparsely as ever. Some have a minimart; some still have a post office. But they each have one, two, or even four churches at their crossroads. When asked where they live, many Piney Woodsians are apt to name one of these hundreds of villages and hamlets.

The question, "Where do you live?" could more aptly be phrased "Where do you belong?" because an unspoken and probably subconscious feeling of belonging to that spot on the globe runs deep. And that feeling – instinct is perhaps a more descriptive word – is a major Piney Woods characteristic that remains unchanged. My great-great grandfather James Eason Russell "acquired" it over 150 years ago. Recall that he and his family migrated from Arkansas to the Piney Woods, stayed awhile, then he moved them back to Arkansas where he soon learned that he liked the Piney Woods better, so back they came. Several years earlier, my triple-great grandfather John P. Renfro probably had the same instinct of belonging when he built one of the first schoolhouses in the county. Mama certainly had it when she asked us to take her back to the Piney Woods to spend her last days. And that same instinct runs in my veins.

Over the years I've worked in many places, some of which struck me as just flat out dreary. Others I liked fine, but something or another about them always made me feel like an outsider. So I cleared a spot on my land that was once Grandpa's cornfield, built a cabin in my woods, and recently moved in full time. I didn't come back expecting a utopia. There are still some trashy places and ignorant people here, but I've seen enough to know the Piney Woods doesn't have a monopoly on that. But I expected to – and did – find my sense of belonging.

Some of my family members share this sense of belonging. An uncle and several of my cousins still live around here. In others though, after many dispersals, it has been diluted, sometimes to the vanishing point. In my immediate family alone, quite a few have followed the technology circuit and become specialists in computers, electronics, the space program, petrochemical design, etc. Others became airline employees who, to paraphrase Grandma, "stay up in the air all day." These kinfolks have lived or worked in California, New York state, Florida, Wyoming, Mexico, India, Singapore, and Paris. As in the old post-World War I song "How Ya Gonna Keep 'Em Down on the Farm After They've Seen Paree?" some of these kinfolks found their niches in big cities and pinto bean areas. And our own family's odyssey is typical of that of many, many other Piney Woodsians.

Of my kinfolks who still feel the tug of the Piney Woods, I'm pretty sure that two or three of them will relocate here someday. Several others who feel 165 years worth of connectedness visit often now, and will continue to do so. I can safely predict that, wherever our future generations are, folks will be laughing and cracking jokes, but I don't want to ponder the future beyond that.

I certainly don't want to hear any more domineering beeps from my computer either. I'm fixin' to shut it down for a mighty long rest, and go roam around in my woods. In my roamings of the past few months, I've found some cedar trees, maples, and hollies that I didn't know were growing on the property. I've found blown-down magnolia leaves that must have come from a tree around here somewhere. And I've found a black gum sapling! I must go sit beside it and maybe even tell it a tale.

ACKNOWLEDGMENTS

As I pondered on all the folks who helped and supported me throughout this writing and publishing process, I could not decide who should be thanked first. So I decided to write their names on individual slips of paper and put them in a hat, then draw each one out randomly.

My friend Marilyn Trujillo's name came out of the hat first. Marilyn and I long ago decided we were sisters who had been separated at birth. Since calling each other "Sis" didn't sound right, we settled on "Ole Buddy." So, many thanks, Ole Buddy, for reviewing my many drafts, making helpful comments, and providing those sudden sparks of inspiration that kept me going. Also I'm beholden to you for searching out reference material on everything from tatting and Liberty ships to shape-note music.

Olivia Tanner's name came out of the hat next. When I was bumbling along, trying to make my first draft presentable, I more and more visualized smashing my computer with a sledgehammer. So I hollered, "Help!" to Olivia, a young lady with all the computer skills of the younger generation. She came to my rescue and soon converted my messy draft into a clean, workable copy, complete with CD and flash drive backup. That original version has now been revised a few times, right up to the final draft. So thank you, Olivia. When you see this in print, I hope it doesn't bring back frustrating memories of having to sort out the earlier mishmash.

Alysia Rebecca Graham's name came out of the hat next. I've watched Alysia, my niece, grow up from Crayola "renderings" posted on the fridge door into an accomplished artist. She's won some top ribbons in juried competitions and is now studying and working to become an even better artist. As perhaps only an auntie can do, I told, rather than asked, her to do the artwork for the family tree and the Texas map. She jumped right in with her own ideas about it and started sketching. I hope you readers agree with me when I say, "Hey, Kiddo, good job."

Gay Nell Rogers Cordes's name came up next. Since she is the granddaughter of Cora Rogers, Grandma's sister, we share Grandma Wade and Pat Sowell as predecessors. By the time I began this book, Gay Nell had already become an avid genealogist. After countless hours of tracking down military and cemetery records and census data from bygone eras, as well as studying genealogy files at Piney Woods libraries, she had traced our lineage on Grandma's side back to the late 1700s. I thank you very much, Gay Nell, for providing me with all this information. It fills many blanks in our family's history. It also provides us with an intriguing mystery about John E. Brown's destiny.

Chuck Bloomquist's name next leaped out of the hat as if to say, "It's my turn." When my manuscript had progressed to the point at which it was ready for a no-holds-barred review, I imposed on Chuck, a systems analyst and history buff, to scrutinize the whole shebang. We had worked together for many years at a consulting firm, figuring out if new, high-tech systems would work like they were supposed to. The final report for each study was always reviewed by a co-worker who acted as devil's advocate, and Chuck and I often reviewed each other's writing from that standpoint. So, in our accustomed fashion, Chuck nitpicked everything from my historical accuracy of Victorianism, Henry Wallace's farm programs, and women's right to vote, to the readability of the book by the general public. Years of putting up with this kind of criticism have not strained our friendship, so I say, "Cheers, Chuck," as I lift at least one glass of wine to you.

The slip of paper that next came out of the hat said, "SFASUpress." These initials spell out Stephen F. Austin State University, which is located right up the road a piece from me in Nacogdoches. SFASU — and its earlier incarnation as SFA Normal College — has long been a member of the composite Piney Woodsian family. In my clan, since back in the Normal College days, many of my cousins earned degrees at SFA, and Mama took summer classes there to keep her teaching credential up to date. Under the directorship of Kimberly Verhines, the SFASU Press is now filling the need to explore the history and culture of the Piney Woods and surrounding areas.

So, Kim, to you and your staff, I thank y'all for guiding me throughout the publishing process. You patiently put up with my countrified ways and unreliable Internet. You responded gently to my, no doubt, silly questions. In the bigger picture, I especially thank y'all for providing a documentation source for information about our unique Piney Woods environment and culture.

I next drew my nephew Russell Graham's name out of the hat. Since shortly after one hectic Christmas Eve night when he was almost born at my house, in true family tradition we've always found something to laugh about. Later on, though, unlike the family tradition, we haven't always shied away from giving each other unasked-for advice. This has never caused the other to get riled up, and it came in mighty handy when manuscript pages and photographs for this book had to be e-mailed here and there.

After some boners on my part, Russell — a bona fide member of the computer generation — pointed out the errors of my ways. He coached me and never (well, almost never) got impatient. Often he pitched right in and handled the transmissions on his own. So, many thanks, Russell, for keeping me from sending things off to unknown locations in the "cloud."

Loretta Russell Kingsley, whose name I drew next, is the daughter of Mama's brother Dale and his wife Jewell, so we share Leah and Eli as common grandparents. Loretta grew up in Oak Flat in the midst of our past and present kinfolks' farmsteads, and she remembers hearing many of the same family tales as I did. During her growing-up years, she spent time with the few old timers who were still with us and was especially close to Grandma Leah. After Grandma's death, the job of going through her trunks, which contained bundles of old letters, documents, and photos, fell upon Loretta's shoulders. She had been interested in genealogy to some extent for quite a while, but sorting through and studying this trove of long-trunk-bound items shifted that interest into high gear.

As thorough as her research was on Grandma's lineage, Loretta joined the ranks of others who could find no details on the final destiny of John E. Brown. She found no such dead ends on Grandpa's side and was able to trace a good bit of that lineage back to much earlier than the 165 years covered in these pages. For instance, she was able to trace James Eason Russell's ancestors back to the 1600s English explorer Henry Hudson (think Hudson Bay and the Hudson River). Loretta generously provided me with all this genealogical information and with many photos. So, as Piney Woodsians say, "Thank you, Loretta, I surely do 'preciate it."

My good friend Diane Ryder's name came out of the hat next. When my final manuscript draft was nearing completion, she agreed to review it. At that point, I had mixed emotions about whether the written words of "my baby" should be set adrift into the wide world of publishing and the general reader, or the pages consigned to the bottom of a birdcage. Diane has a degree in economics and worked in that field before entering seminary and becoming an ordained minister. She is also an ex-New Yorker, an avid reader, and a wordsmith par excellence. Thus I knew she would give me her totally honest opinion, and in New Yorkers' typical way, would not sugarcoat it. Her short-and-to-the-point comments on the draft set my mind at ease about turning "my baby" loose on its own. So, many thanks, Diane, for your continuing support and encouragement —

and for saving my manuscript from a birdcage.

The slip of paper with Ann Applegarth's name came out of the hat last. We've been friends through thick and thin forever and a day. She's an English major, has long taught poetry classes, and is also an accomplished writer. Her works include a novela, short stories, and poems, including Western poetry that conjures up images of the sights, sounds, and action of rodeos and roundups, and the coming-of-age experiences of ranchers' young'uns. As an added plus, she spent a lot of her growing-up years in East Texas, so knows how folks in the area think, act, and talk.

Ann has supported and encouraged me in many ways since quite early in this book's progress. She edited each "generation" of the manuscript and suggested good ways to improve wording. She corrected my lousy spelling and fixed dangling participles. She made sure my words were safely and correctly stored in electronic memory. I thank you heartily, Ann. After the many, many hours you've spent on all this, I'm sure you now know the manuscript as well as I do. Although your name came out of the hat last, if I ever start handing out "Black Gum award statuettes," you'll be the first to get one!

www.ingramcontent.com/pod-product-compliance
Lightning Source LLC
Chambersburg PA
CBHW071200070526
44584CB00019B/2868